From Vic :)

March 2013

Being happy

Vic Gilgeous, PhD

Lulu.com

ISBN 978-1-4709–3869-7

First Edition

© 2011 by Vic Gilgeous

All rights reserved. No part of this publication may be reproduced or transmitted in any form or by any means, electronic or mechanical, including photocopy, recording or any information storage and retrieval system without the prior written permission of both the copyright owner and the publisher of this first edition.

British Library Cataloguing in Publication Data

A catalogue record for this book is available from the British Library.

Layout in Book Antiqua 12pt

This edition published via www.LULU.com

Contents

Introduction..7

Happiness works!...................................13

What is happiness? 19

What happiness is to me.......................27

Important questions about happiness..................29

How happy are you?.............................. 41

What is the point of happiness? 45

Happiness truths 49

What you can do to be happier

See past your thoughts..59

You can choose happiness................................... 73

Practice appreciation..81

Chill and enjoy life..99

Be authentic...105

Get some passion in your life...........................121

Have more fun! 137

Be in touch with who you really are....................151

Imprint the ideas of happiness into your subconscious 165

Being happy and practicing happiness 177

A plan for your continued happiness 189

Tying things up 193

Acknowledgments 201

About the author 203

Other work by the author................................ 205

References..207

Introduction

Continued unhappiness, for whatever reason, just eats away your life. It is like being trapped without any chance of escape. This was how I once felt. Wanting to feel better, I went to my local night class and enrolled on a course in happiness. To my surprise, and delight, it worked. I became much happier. I learnt that the reasons for my unhappiness were not unique to me. This means that although there are numerous, and, for each person, different reasons as to why they are upset, the good news is there are just a few identifiable causes of anyone's malaise. This means it is always possible to turn off anyone's unhappiness tap.

Many people think they are blighted because they have never really been a happy person anyway. Conversations run this way. "I'm the same as others in our family. None of us have really been cheerful people; I think it is in our genes, we are just born that way." Modern validated research shows that people, who think they have had a happiness bypass surgery, still have a happiness center in their brain. And, it is possible for them to lastingly attain what can only be described as exceptionally high happiness levels.

We can become unhappy when we miss the mark in terms of what we expect to happen with situations in our life. To become happier our personality sets out its stall to be more successful in the future. Trouble comes if the personality is never happy in the now, because it thinks there is always something it lacks. This is called being fearful. What's more, future success is always a myth if the journey towards it is fraught with misery. This is called being unhappy. Such fear and unhappiness don't exist when you live from the real truth which is:

> *'Success cannot guarantee real happiness, but happiness can.'*

Yet the message of fear and unhappiness are still peddled by the newspapers, the television, our parents, teachers, and others, who tell us that it's a difficult world out there. We can see why many focus on what is wrong, and dwell on misfortunes and hardship. Once you sing the song, "I am upset, life is bad for me, and I hope things don't get worse," you unwittingly put yourself in danger. You do so because:

> *'What you focus on is what you bring into your life.'*

This means if you focus on old wounds, grievances, guilt, and, in fact, any low emotions, you will always end up attracting more of the same into your life. Whereas, if your focus is one of happiness; meaning you are mindful of love, joy, abundance, appreciation, friendship and kindness, then these things will start to appear in your life with greater and greater frequency. What's more, validated clinical research shows that besides being more successful, happier people live longer, have better emotional and physical health, are more creative, and have better relationships.

This book goes into more detail on what I have just discussed and, because it is known that the more awareness you have of happiness the happier you will become, you are provided with what the prominent writers on happiness have to say. This is followed by explanations and stories which show you that being happy is an inside job.

The meat of the book provides you with the following ten proven ways to be happy:

1. *See past your thoughts*
2. *You can choose happiness*
3. *Practice appreciation*
4. *Chill and enjoy life*
5. *Be authentic*
6. *Get some passion in your life*
7. *Have more fun!*
8. *Being in touch with who you really are*
9. *Imprint the ideas of happiness into your subconscious*
10. *Being happy and practicing happiness*

You are shown practical ways to align with your real self which, despite life's ups and downs, is always there to give you contentment. This brings your attention back to your authenticity, your wisdom and compassion, which always contributes to yours and everyone's wellness.

The good news is that you do not have to do this on your own. Your heightened consciousness opens you to receiving the universal power and wisdom of Spirit. The right support, people, and resources will appear in your life. This is the fulfillment this book brings to you; that of being happy, realising your passion for being the best you can be, and being able to move around this Earth to spread to others the love and joy that is already in you.

Vic Gilgeous

Nottingham

November 2011

Happiness works!

When you are down and feel as if life is against you, *'being happy'* is possible. It works! Because when you are being happy, your life does get better! Let me explain.

There was a time in my life when I felt very depressed and miserable. "This can't be me", I told myself, "I should feel fine, I have good health, a good career, and a great wife." I knew something was wrong, and it had to be fixed.

I think I thought if I could be more successful in my life, then I would be happier. I kind of then proclaimed to myself, and anything out there that could listen, "There has to be something, or somebody, that can help me." Time passed and I spotted that the university I worked for ran, for ten evenings, a course on happiness. I signed up. I even bought a booklet on jokes, since I thought this course would be something like a Ken Dodd show. What I was to learn really did surprise me.

So, there I was, on the happiness course, being told by the tutor what real happiness is. It was so strange; even half way through the first session; something was starting to happen to me. I was becoming different deep inside. It felt as if I had landed on another planet, where the ideas and ways of going about things were totally different from anything I knew. The weeks passed, and on the third week I had to find out what was going on. At the end of the session, when everyone else had gone, I asked the tutor question after question about happiness. He patiently listened, but brought my quizzing to an end in the most brilliant fashion. He walked me to the board, and wrote on it these words, "**IT WORKS!**"

At this point I need to tell you that I had been a University lecturer for years. I knew the ropes, I was considered be a good teacher, but I couldn't fathom out how the tutor on this happiness course was doing what he did. I was actually becoming happy!

I had got to know the caretaker of the building, and, one night asked him if he would do me a favour. "After the break, could you stand outside the door and see what you think is going on. We all seem to be getting happier, and I can't work out what he is doing. Perhaps he is hypnotising us?"

At the end of the session I managed to find the caretaker and asked him if he had listened. He had, and said it had quite puzzled him. "What do you mean", I asked. "Well, the tutor says such and such, and, with no more ado, somebody in the class says, oh thank you, yes, I'm now sorted! I don't get what he does, but I'm only the caretaker."

It was then that the penny dropped for me. "Yes", I replied. "What you say about what is going on is just that. The tutor says very little about how to be happy, yet we become happy. I've got it! Something happens in the middle, between him saying something, and someone becoming happy. That something that happens is, he offers a way of looking at things differently, and being different, in order to be happier. But it is up to us to see how it can work, when we apply it to our own situation. Each of us has to see for ourselves that things can become better. When we do, this becomes our new natural way to be happy." The caretaker scratched his head and went about his business.

I can now tell you more about this. What I was learning was that my old ways of looking at things had kept me miserable. For example, it was not my beliefs that were the culprit. They were there anyway. It was my attachment to my beliefs that I needed to drop; especially those about life that made me angry, and made me feel low. It was my dogged adherence to solving these low thoughts which drove my decisions, and kept me battling with my fears. This continually distanced me from the happiness that was already inside of me. I was being prompted by the tutor to realise I could choose to think, and be different, in ways that let the happiness I already had shine through. One of the wonderful things I experienced was this:

'Success cannot guarantee real happiness, but happiness can.'

The tutors name is Henry Wittka-Jezewska; what a great teacher of happiness. Also, I have learnt so much from Hay House Radio, in particular the works of Robert Holden PhD and Dr Wayne Dyer. Because of this my life has changed in so many wonderful ways.

I am still lucky enough to have my lovely wife, who shares my passion for happiness. Like everyone, I have my ups and downs, but there is always an underlying happiness I can lean on. In fact, I can describe this more often than not as bliss.

For many years now I have presented my own happiness courses. In this book I offer you ways of being happy that will give you a great life.

What is happiness?

What I am telling you is that you can be much happier than you presently are. If you feel you are an unredeemable misery, or that you are already happy enough, it is now known that it is always possible for your happiness level to be raised. How is this so? It is not a secret. It is simple. It is about knowing more than you now know about happiness. Let me explain this in a different way.

With a guide you get more

When I holiday somewhere I have not visited before, I love to just mooch around, looking at what takes my interest. Whilst this is pleasant, if I can, I get on a guided tour. This way, I quickly get to know stuff normally hidden from me, like historical information and local areas of interest. As a result I appreciate the place more than I normally would, and, I enjoy my visit more.

In the same way, a guide is necessary if you are to come away with more than a superficial look at what happiness is. The more you know about happiness, the more you can experience happiness. It is about knowing what happiness is, how it can be attained, and why it can sometimes seem to be absent. What I am talking about in this book is being happier through the practice of being happy in oneself; made possible by an awareness of what happiness is.

So, your awareness of happiness, that is, getting a deeper idea of what happiness is, is a big key to you being happy. When you raise your consciousness about happiness, you start to shift your perspective. That is, you start to look at life through a different lens. Such a lens sees love instead of fear, and peace instead of fighting.

When you do this much of life's daily problems will seem less of a burden and your present level of happiness will grow. This happiness will become deeper, and it will last.

'The more awareness you have of happiness, the happier you will become.'

Definitions of happiness can help here

Here are snapshots of what three prominent exponents of happiness say:

Martin Seligman[1]

Seligman through extensive surveys has found that happiness is dependent on the following:

Your biological parents. How happy or otherwise your biological parents were.

Your circumstances. Certain circumstances can sometimes change happiness for the better. Examples being: marriage, social life, striving to experience less negative emotions, and religion.

How satisfied you are with your past. Your joys, sorrows, regrets, and success.

Your happiness in the present. Your joy, ecstasy, calm, zest, ebullience, pleasure and flow with life.

Your optimism about the future. Your optimism, hope, faith and trust.

Deepak Chopra[2]

Deepak Chopra makes use of Seligman's model of happiness, but emphasises that the cause of our suffering lies in our ignorance of not knowing who we really are. He expounds on the following revelations which, if we bring to the forefront of our consciousness, can bring us happiness:

"Who you are transcends space, time, and cause-and-affect. Your core consciousness is immortal.

In finding the place where your true self resides the secret of happiness will unfold.

Any step you take toward your core consciousness – your ground state, your true self – obliterates some causes of unhappiness in your life, allowing your innate happiness to blossom."

Robert Holden[3]

Robert talks about happiness falling into three main categories. And, informs us how an appreciation of these three *"types"* of happiness is very helpful for understanding the nature of true happiness. They are:

1. *Pleasure*. The name we give to the happiness we experience through our physical senses. It is what makes for a good time.

2. *Satisfaction*. The name given to the type of happiness that comes from getting what we want, or enjoying circumstances and conditions that are deemed favourable. Other words to describe this happiness include 'contentment', 'fulfilment', and 'well-being'.
3. *Joy*. Joy is the soul of happiness. Like satisfaction, it can be felt emotionally and appreciated mentally, but it is much more than an emotion or a state of mind. Other words to describe this type of happiness include 'bliss' and 'ecstasy'. Unless we cultivate an awareness of joy, no amount of pleasure or satisfaction can make us happy.

Summary so far

The main lesson here is that you will become happier the more you focus your attention on what happiness is. Affirmations on happiness can help with this. When you speak them out aloud, or think them in your head, they embed themselves in your consciousness. As a result your life will focus more on the ways of happiness.

Here are four affirmations you can make:
1. *I am taking more and more interest in what real happiness is.*
2. *I am seeking what the good writers and speakers have to say on the topic of happiness.*
3. *I am practicing being happier.*
4. *I am becoming happier.*

What happiness is to me

I know I am happy when I feel good. To me this is when I am being myself, just being content and appreciating what is here in the moment. At other times it is looking forward to something I enjoy, or doing something specific which I enjoy; like being, with my wife, friends, at the theatre, at the gym, doing yoga and eating out. Just as important to my happiness is working on something I find purposeful, like teaching happiness.

What is equally important to my happiness is dealing with moments when I feel bad. This can happen when life deals me a blow. It can be because I am not happy with my self-image, or when I dwell on past issues, or worry about the future. I now know this is about my beliefs, and hence the way I think.

Fortunately, as you will learn here, there are ways of being happy that defuse any thoughts and beliefs that can bring us so much misery.

Because of this, I feel there is a sense of peace in my life. My moods are generally good, and reflect a helpful attitude towards myself, others, life and the world. For me happiness is a feeling like, *"I feel good, everything is okay."* Sometimes it goes further than this, in the sense that I do sometimes feel blissful. Yes, it comes and goes, but I do know it is there, and it is capable of coming back again. So, from being happy, to sometimes being blissful, is the gift of this knowingness of happiness I give to you in this book.

Important questions about happiness

Sometimes we can't even make a start on being happy if we think we are born not so happy, and there is nothing we can do about it. Some of my students have said, "What's wrong with just seeking pleasure and getting stuff. After all, life is so short?" Other people have said, "I keep searching for ways to be happy, and end up just going round in circles." The best one is. "I'm not stupid. I've analysed my upsets this way and that, but I still haven't managed to get rid of them."

What follows provides answers these sorts of comments.

Does the way we are affect our happiness?

Researchers say we each have a set point in our brain which is responsible for approximately 40 percent of our experience of happiness. It is said that this is mainly genetic, but also childhood influences play a part. So, it might seem that a sticking point on yours, or anyone's happiness, is that we each have a built in propensity for happiness. Perhaps that is why some people always seem to be upbeat and happy, whilst others can seem to be miserable and unhappy. If we consider our level of happiness to be the result of our makeup when we came into this world, and if we consider ourselves to be somewhat miserable or downbeat, is there any hope of us ever being happy? If so, this answer is valuable.

'Even if you are a bona-fide, fully paid up member of some misery club, it is still possible for you to become very happy.'

Programmes which have focused on improving people's level of happiness have found that people who have a low set point, or base level, of happiness can significantly raise their happiness levels to levels well above the population norm. Specifically, on completion of such programmes, happiness scales are used to test the levels of happiness of the attendees. In many cases the people tested were found to have attained significantly high scores of happiness. More encouragingly, months, and years later, when these individuals were re-tested, these higher levels of happiness were shown to be evident.

Is pleasure and our circumstances the key to happiness?

We all look forward to enjoying life's pleasures. Sometimes when life gets miserable, our pleasures can sometimes seem to be the only way out. But, if pleasure was the answer to being happy in life, many pleasure seekers, and people with good conditions of living, would be continually happy. This is not the case.

Pleasure is a transitory thing. What can cause us to feel good can go away, and we can feel down until we get some more of it. Sometimes we can become desensitised to a continuance of the same pleasure, or we can start to feel bored and in want of another type of pleasure. In this way the happiness we get has peaks and troughs. Such happiness that comes and goes, and sometimes bores us, is not *real happiness*. If we can, another way to become happier is to improve the conditions of our life. Things like housing, health, and relationships, spring to mind here. But again, it has been shown that such changes initially boost our happiness, but after a while we revert back to our previous happiness level. In any case the research shows that our life circumstances account for approximately 10 percent of the total happiness experience.

In the end, is our happiness up to us?

The good news is that apparently almost 50 percent of our happiness is down to the choices we can make with our lives. Everyone is different, and our happiness can centre on things to do with being loving, having meaning and purpose in our lives, making use of our main strengths - our creative expression, and helping others.

Certainly, knowing more and more about happiness will bring out the happiness which is always there in you. When you raise your consciousness around happiness you will feel happier in yourself and naturally attract sources of happiness in the outside world. And, the more you know, even if it is modest, the happier you will become. It is a bit like this: *"Wedge your foot in the door; if you keep pushing, it will open to show you all your happiness."* But, if you still feel that happiness, so far, has eluded you, it can help if you know that the Spirit of happiness is already in you. If you are poetically inclined and want to delve into the sacred source of your happiness, look up the wonderful verses from the sacred Persian poet Hafiz[4], (c1320-1389). Hafiz knows where your happiness hides. These two lines from one of his poems sum this up beautifully:

'We should talk about this problem'
"There is a Beautiful Creature Living in a hole you have dug."

"We should talk about this problem."

Can the way we think make us happy or unhappy?

A major factor that emerges when we consider our happiness is how we use our mind. The Dalai Lama says: *"We have a mind, which is all the basic equipment we need to achieve complete happiness. Anxious thoughts can lead to depression and thoughts of anger and hatred do destroy us."* The fact is, for many of us, happiness is just an illusion because we spend a lot of our time in our head mulling over regrets and guilt about the past, and worrying about what the future could bring. The trouble is, such low level thoughts can become an ingrained way of thinking. This results in giving us a low level of life energy which, if continued, will make us ill. Also, it is difficult to make decent decisions about helpful possibilities in your life, when your head is not clear because it is full of unhelpful thoughts. The way out of this is to notice that you are having such debilitating thoughts. Then, knowing that examining such thoughts keeps you tied to them, disabling you from moving on in favour of noticing the good things and possibilities that are happening in your life right now.

In most cases low thoughts spring from beliefs we have about life that are not serving us well. So, since the way we think is based on our beliefs then it follows that an important aspect of getting in touch with our happiness is to ask ourselves, "Are my beliefs serving me well?" As we shall see, any beliefs that give rise to anger, hopelessness, jealousy, fear, being separate from others, or other such low emotions, means you are self-creating your own suffering. In any case, whether or not you see that at this moment, any unhelpful beliefs are not in accord with the reality that things are always in your favour

The irony is now clear. We are all given the human gift of the capacity to think and imagine. We can use this gift to assume what it will be like for us when we are happier, and are helping others to be happy. Sadly we often overlook this way of thinking, and engage in low thoughts, with the result that we bring suffering upon ourselves and others.

Summary so far

The main lesson here is that no matter what your current level of happiness is, it is possible to improve it significantly, very quickly. And, the happiness realised is real happiness, which is lasting. Unhappiness can arise when you discover that the happiness you get from the outside world does not last, or is taken from you. Your personality always suffers when this happens. This can feel like a permanent blow, until you realise two things:

1. Your personality does, on occasions, enter miserable valleys. If you choose to stay there, woe betide. But, if you choose to move on, you will naturally move towards the helpful possibilities that lie in the uplands.
2. You are much more than your personality. Your unconditioned self, which has always been there, which you can always connect with, is filled with love and happiness.

Again, affirmations on happiness can help here. When you take the effort to speak them out aloud, or think them in your head, over time, they reinforce an empowering attitude of well-being into your sub consciousness. And, since your sub conscious is the Satnav of your thinking, this means your thoughts and emotions will project a happier you. In turn, you will find that all aspects of your life will improve.

Here are three affirmations you can make:
1. *I am seeking ways to improve my happiness and notice the improvement they make.*
2. *Beyond the normal pleasures of life I am looking for ways to be, and think, which will bring me continued peace, fulfilment and happiness.*
3. *More and more I am looking for the essence of who I am in order to be authentic and happy in my life.*

How happy are you?

How happy are you generally? The happiness questionnaire below can help you roughly assess how happy you are.

Happiness questionnaire

Below are eight questions asking how you feel about your circumstances now, the outside world, others you know, how your life has panned out, and what you think about the future. For each question give a score based on the following answers:

1 = Definitely not.

2 = Not so much.

3 = Neutral.

4 = More or less.

5 = Very much so.

Questions:

1. I am proud of where I live
2. I appreciate the people in my life
3. I laugh a lot
4. I feel safe when I go out
5. I think the world is a good place
6. I am looking forward to my future
7. I have few regrets about my life
8. I am comfortable with myself and the way things are

What happiness category are you in?

33 – 40 = You are very happy with your life.

25 – 32 = You are fairly positive about your life.

17– 24 = You are neither unduly positive or unhappy with your life.

9 – 16 = You are not so pleased with your life in general.

1 – 8 = You are very unhappy with your life.

Your view on happiness

Having just been supplied with some food for thought, the following four questions can be useful for improving your level of happiness.

1. Does your score agree with how happy you feel about your life?
2. Are there aspects of your life you think might be the cause of any unhappiness?
3. What aspects of your life make you happy?
4. What do you think happiness now means to you?

What is the point of happiness?

Modern validated clinical research shows there is much to be gained from being happy:

'Happier people live longer, have better emotional and physical health, are more creative, more successful, and have better relationships. They think clearer, feel more confident, and make better decisions.'

I think, "Wow"! Since simply being happy is more than enough for me!

More good stuff about happiness

Happy thoughts will release endorphins and dopamine into your body and this will make you feel good. You will sleep better, and better sleep produces happiness. When you are truly happy you are radiant, you notice life more, appreciate things and feel more abundant. In particular, when you are happy, you will find that people like you more and act positively towards you, though they may not know why.

Everything can seem so rich, so clear, bright and wonderful

Many years ago, a friend of mine, who had lost his wife to Motor Neurone Disease, remarried to a lovely lady who had lost her husband to cancer. After the wedding he told me how astoundingly good everything felt. He said, "Everything seems so rich, clear, bright and wonderful; my bride, the people, the wedding, the reception, the weather … everything."

He certainly was floating. I know that type of feeling, and you don't have to have come through an ordeal, or be in love to have it. It's as if everything is all right with the world. You feel free, loved, and can think clearly. You know what it is you want, and why you are here on this earth.

This happiness is innate; you don't have to learn it. You just need to be reminded that being happy is your natural state. You were not born miserable, but you can let your circumstances, others, and the world make you so. Also there will be times when, as they do, things go terribly wrong for you, and, in that moment of it happening, of course it is awful. But, it is always possible to remain grounded in your happiness. In this state, life's inevitable travails seem less daunting, and you know you are going to overcome the situation and move on. The bonus is that you can, and will want to, spread happiness to others. This means you become closer to those you meet, and will see more clearly that their troubles, in most part, are because of the way their thoughts lead them.

Happiness truths

What if scientists discovered a super vaccine that could cure most illnesses and diseases? It might seem a bit far-fetched that this could happen, but let's hope that in time it could. Perhaps scientists could discover what could be done to make people happy. This is an equally lofty ideal, since the outcome would be just the same; people would live longer, be more creative, more successful and more fulfilled. Just imagine that the scientists had discovered how to make people happy. If so, what do you think they would say needs to be done? What secrets might be revealed? Let me tell you now that such wishful thinking is unnecessary, since the truth of happiness holds no secrets. When we look to the timeless wisdom that has been available to us through the ages, the way of happiness, as explained below, is clearly revealed.

The pursuit of happiness is an illusion

Happiness is not something to be pursued, something that has to be earned, to do with luck, circumstances, or what we have. Often happiness is associated with the state of mind that we think we will have when we **put our life right.** This means we are telling ourselves, we can't really be happy until this future state is attained. For example, people say, "I'll be happy when … I'm qualified, get that job, get that car, get married", and so on. Do you see yourself here? Perhaps you can add to this list. If happiness depended on these things, then those that have it all should be really happy. And, we know this is not the case. Happiness is not about stuff. Numerous research studies have shown that pursuing things have not brought people increased happiness. The drawback is that usually, we have to spend a lot of effort and time, sometimes doing soul destroying work, to acquire these things. The double whammy is:

1. When we get more of anything, for example, praise, possessions, promotions, our expectations are raised, we want more. And, when we get it, we may have to tie up time and money in order to keep it, and maintain its value.
2. When we look at others who have more, we may start to think that what we have is not enough, and therefore, we again want more. So, the cycle of wanting more, and having to jump through hoops to get it, is perpetuated.

The root of this problem lies deep in our psyche, our fear of scarcity. Our natural reaction is to hunt for what we think we need. The trouble is that even if we get what we want, we think it will not last, and off we go again. We can become so busy that we have insufficient time left to enjoy and appreciate life.

Having said all this, it is fair to say that life programmes us to chase after stuff and we feel better if we have stuff. The problem arises when we become so attached to stuff that it drives our life. We stop being driven when we know that, *'we are in charge of our happiness, not stuff.'* This being the case, the following mantra can be of help:

'When what we think we need holds less attraction to us; it no longer has any hold over us.'

Your happiness is already here

Here we are then with the facts of life; all the things external to you like, money, situation, possessions, circumstances, position, friends, lovers, relationships, and so on, do not come with a guarantee. They cannot be guaranteed to stay as part of your life. The outside world, we all know, changes. Everything has a season and life has its ups as well as downs. Does this then leave your happiness down to the vagaries of life? And, what about if you feel your situation is unbearable and impossible to change. Are you doomed to unhappiness or misery? The answer to both these questions is, "No"!

If you are to experience real lasting happiness, a fundamental change to your understanding and approach to happiness is needed. You can choose to look for it outside yourself. Certainly the brainwashing we receive from society and the media keeps us looking for happiness outside ourselves. This is looking for happiness in the wrong places, and, often this can be a costly experience. A quotation by Hosea Ballou[5] expresses this perfectly:

"Real happiness is cheap enough, yet how dearly we pay for its counterfeit."

Nonetheless, those without stuff, or who live in very difficult circumstances with very little chance to change things would certainly say that happiness is difficult to find. This does not mean that all is lost. When all outside options fail and you cannot change anything outside yourself to make yourself happy, you will finally come to see that the only thing you have that can be changed to bring you happiness is *you*.

'Your happiness is in you and always has been.'

'Happiness is your inherent nature.'

The power to become happy is in your own hands. Like the air we breathe, happiness is free, it needs no reason. For example, do children need a reason to laugh; do you need a reason to buy flowers? It is you who has the choice for happiness. You can choose to be happy. When you do this you join with the happiness that does not change at all, the happiness that is within you all the time. Consider this golden lesson:

> *'Happiness comes when you go inside, instead of looking for it outside of yourself.'*

This means that when you do things in the world that comes from your heart and is joyful, you will be happy. In other words, you know you can still get happiness from outside things you like. One simple thing I like is having a drink of great coffee. But, you need to remember that many people, in order to be happy, strive for more money, or approval, or power, and such. And, to do this they have to drink poison.

You are in the best place for happiness

I learnt this from my grandfather. When I was a kid I use to spend a lot of time at his house. He only lived two doors away, at 153 Woodcock Street. When I got thirsty and asked for a drink he would fill a glass of water from the tap, give it to me and say, "You will enjoy that, the best water in the world comes from 153 Woodcock Street."

One day, when I was at home, I told my mum that I was thirsty and was going to my grandfather's house for a drink. She looked puzzled and said to me, "What do you mean, just get a drink from the tap."

My instant reply, which made her laugh, was, "It's not as good as the water at granddad's house; the best water in the world comes from 153 Woodcock Street."

As I grew up I looked back on my behaviour then and thought of the wisdom my grandfather had passed down to me. You see, my grandfather had been a navigator and had sailed all over the world. He had been twice shipwrecked, and had saved lives. He certainly had experienced adventure and seen the world. He told me, from his worldly perspective, that 153 Woodcock Street was the best place in the world to be. Therefore, the best water in the world comes from the same place.

We can all take this lesson on board when it comes to happiness. That is, you can go all over the place in search of finding happiness, but what you can find, if you look for it, is that happiness is right where you are. It is inside you, in the way you think and the way that you are. So the key lesson I can reiterate here is:

'Happiness is already here, it comes from you.'

This naturally feels contrary to what our senses tell us. This is because our minds have been conditioned to believe in what the adverts say; get a great life, get a great car, get a great body, and so on. Consequently we may not feel we are okay unless we have the trappings to prove we are really okay. If this is the case then we are admitting, perhaps unwittingly, that we are not okay with ourselves.

What you can do to be happier

What follows are ten powerful and effective ways to help you become happier.

1. See past your thoughts

Our essential being always is happy, but this is obscured when our thoughts make us feel troubled. Such thoughts could be about wanting and expecting more, issues with the past, trying to establish the right conditions for happiness, concerns about the future, and so on.

> *'Sometimes people are so unhappy you would think they were connected by wires to someone, or something, that was administering them electric shocks every now and then. We need to remember we are not connected to anything, only our thoughts.'*

When we think about something, we project it out there into the world, and this is fed back to us and becomes the reality we experience. It is like we wear a pair of special spectacles which continually runs a film of the things we think. Because of this, when we look at the world, we do not see what is really out there. Our thoughts intervene to interpret what is out there. What we see is not reality, but the film of our thoughts. If our thoughts run a scary or unhelpful film, we will feel threatened and miserable. Even if the film is a nice one, we must remember, it is not what is actually going on in the outside world; it is our thoughts. I must point out that:

'It is not actually our thoughts that are the problem; it is what we think about our thoughts.'

If we let them make us miserable they will. If we believe they are true, we are mistaken. They are just our thoughts. When we become used to standing back from our thoughts, we do two things.

1. We connect with our inherent wisdom and happiness, and we see people and the world in a more clear and honest way.
2. We can make use of any unhelpful thoughts to show us that unless we look at things differently, it will be difficult for our happiness to shine through.

Believing your low thoughts will perpetuate misery

A hypnotherapy client explained to me why he was so annoyed and frustrated with everything. It went like this … *"My parents, particularly my father, were never on my side. He did not understand me. This caused a lot of fights, and I mean real fights. Sometimes teeth were broken and noses were bloodied."*

The client was in his seventies, and this took place when he was an adolescent.

After more discourse on this, he then changed to talk about his career.

"Despite my best efforts, I was not valued at work. Others always seemed to get the promotions and recognition. Even when I doubled my efforts, certain individuals took the credit for what I did. All in all I was given a rough deal, especially by the management. Time after time, I showed the ways that management were out of touch. Even worse, they lied and pulled rank to get their way. This just left me feeling frustrated. I really felt as if the system, and those at the top, had no idea of how to motivate anyone. It was stifling and I was not appreciated."

At this time the client had been retired from work for ten years. I asked him what had happened with him more recently.

"I joined a local community welfare group. It was a voluntary thing. At the group meetings certain people there, who were genuinely trying to help, were made scapegoats when things didn't go to plan. I made my views clear, only to find that those in charge turned against me. This all seemed so stupid a way to go on. All this in fighting and waste of energy, when all we were supposed to be doing was helping the community."

I looked at the client. He looked drawn; his face visibly portrayed bitterness and misery. I knew, over the years, a lot of the time, his thoughts must have placed him in hell.

I tried to stop the client going through more instances of when things had upset him.

I asked him if he thought there was a pattern behind why he thought these types of things had happened. He said he didn't really understand what I meant by that, unless I was suggesting that he had been in the wrong, and not others. He then went over again some of the incidents he had referred to, and emphasised that he had insights into why things had gone wrong, that others either didn't or did not wish to see. He emphasised the point that when he railed against this type of thing he ended up being treated badly. It was all so unfair. People just didn't seem to understand him. Again, he asked me if I thought he was lying, or at least exaggerating, and perhaps painting a more blown up picture of his righteousness in all this.

Having listened to him, I said I thought his points were valid. I then asked him how he felt about these thoughts, that for years and years had gone around and around in his head.

"It's like being in the midst of a bloody battle that never ends. I keep going over the pros and cons of things in order to make any sense of it all. After all, these things

actually did happen? Am I supposed to just blank them out?"

I told him that other clients had experienced similar problems, but, I had helped them to get peace in their life; not by going over their thoughts, but by starting to see that their thoughts were just that, thoughts. If they didn't give attention and emphasis to their thoughts, they would see, over time, their mind would start to settle and their life would start to feel better.

"But they are my thoughts and it is really upsetting to have them. How is it possible to stop these thoughts, when these things actually did happen? Am I supposed to just blank them out," he responded.

I explained that some people have neutral thoughts, some pleasant, and some, like his, are upsetting. We are all like that, but it is the upsetting thoughts that we need to respond to differently, because, if we don't we will make ourselves ill. I said that if he were to consider what I had to say next, and put it into practice, he would see his life starting to change for the better almost immediately.

"It's as if you have painted in your mind a picture filled with unsettling and horrible scenes. Quite frequently, because it has become a habit, you project this picture onto a screen in your mind, and you look at it. And, every time you do, it upsets you. In an attempt to put things right, you analyse the picture and this never works. In fact, it just seems to perpetuate the misery. Other people who see such a picture may choose to switch to a better picture, one filled with happier memories. Or they may simply choose to do something else that takes their mind off the picture. But, the best way to cure people, who constantly find they are looking at a terrible picture, is to get them to understand the picture for what it is. It is just a picture. My advice to you is to try doing this. It works.

Understand that it may be cathartic to go into what happened in order to understand things. Maybe you can even have a good cry. But, do not fall into the trap that sorting out the ins and outs, and rights and wrongs, of what is in the picture will help stop the misery. It won't. I emphasise again, what will sort things out is realising the picture is not real. It is just a picture. It is a picture that upsets you. Stop getting involved with the picture. If you don't, it will eventually ruin you. It will drag you down; make you miserable and ill, and a difficult person to be with.

The reason why this will happen is because the picture you see is based on your thoughts, and when you really believe in them, they will always keep showing up in your life. If you believe ... you are not valued ... life is unfair ... people at the top are incompetent ... in the past you were treated badly ... your talents are not recognised ... others cheat ... the world is a harsh place, and so on, then this is what you will experience. Instances and events will keep showing up in your life whereby you will experience ... people not valuing you ... people treating you unfairly ... being the victim of people in charge who are incompetent ... people treating you badly ... your abilities and worth being overlooked ... being cheated on ... life being harsh to you ... In other words, accepting your low thoughts as true, you will attract into your life negative events, situations and people. What you say is the way things are is just what will turn up for you.

The running of any picture at the front of your mind obscures what is really happening in front of you in real life. When you take your attention off the picture, you will start to see the world as it really is. You will be more present and authentic. In this way you will find your relationships and communication with others will improve. The middle man agenda of your thoughts will stop being in the way. Try doing this. Try realising it is not your thoughts themselves, but your belief and focussed attention on them that causes you trouble.

Please reflect on all this and come back and see me. I cannot do all this for you. It has to be done by you."

The next time I saw this client he looked much brighter. This is what he said.

"I have taken on board many of the things you said to me. I now see how my attachment to my thoughts had steered me off course. Now my life has stopped being blighted by the type of things that use to always turn up. As a result, my moods have lifted and I am seeing the world in all sorts of wonderful ways. I am definitely happier and feel much freer and able to be myself."

The lessons here are:
- We sometimes project a horrible picture onto a screen in our mind. When we really believe

in them, they will always keep showing up in our life.
- The picture, is just a picture, it is not real. It obscures what is really happening in front of us in real life.
- It is not our thoughts themselves, but our belief and focussed attention on them that cause us trouble.
- We need to stop getting involved with the picture. If we don't, it will drag us down.
- Paying attention to low thoughts will attract more of the same into our life.
- Constantly going over what has upset us will not bring good solutions or make us happy.
- Lifting our thoughts, or just letting upsetting thoughts pass by, will give us a better chance of living a happier life.
- Going quiet to our thoughts lets our wisdom give us a knowing of what is best for us.

Here are six affirmations you can make:

1. *I am aware that a focus on low thoughts can lead to misery and illness.*
2. *I am aware that my belief and focussed attention on certain thoughts can keep me stuck in life.*
3. *I am always open to the wisdom I have.*
4. *I am not attached to what my thoughts would lead me to believe is real.*
5. *I am open to being present and authentic in my life.*
6. *I am looking for events and situations that make me happy.*

2. You can choose happiness

You can choose to be happy or miserable. If something goes wrong, you might see it as an opportunity to do things differently, others might decide that it's time to put their head in the gas oven.

It is up to us how we react to the good and bad in our life. If we want to take responsibility for our own happiness, we need to exercise our choice to concentrate on what is working and good, rather than on what is going wrong. Some people, when they are insulted by others, will carry on the hurt for years, whilst the other person involved may have long forgotten what they said. Other people decide to move their thoughts on, instead of dwelling on insults and past hurts. Some of us find this is difficult to do, and we can be left feeling miserable.

But, it is not the situation here that causes us to feel bad; it is our thoughts about the situation. Knowing this means we can make use of the following truism:

'Our emotions and our reality are determined by our thoughts, not the other way round.'

So, when the next thing happens that makes us feel bad, we know it is happening because it is our bad thoughts that are upsetting us. Because this is not what we want we have to concede that we have been letting our thoughts, in effect, run our life. This all can be stopped when we decide to react differently to such thoughts. We do this when we step back from our thoughts. After all, they are just thoughts. When we do this we will discover that bad thoughts don't give us grief if we don't keep focusing on them.

You free yourself from hurt when you realise that it is you, not others, who torture you. So keep in mind:

> *'You can be a victim of your thoughts, unless you stop dwelling on them.'*
>
> *'Nobody can make you feel anything.'*

This then is good news for you, in that, any thoughts that bring you misery and unhappiness can prompt you to do things differently. You can take your focus off such thoughts and decide to be happy, starting from today.

You can decide to be happy

In the film 'The Pursuit of Happyness', Chris Gardner, played by Will Smith, is a bright and talented, but unsuccessful salesman. This film is based on the life of Christopher Paul Gardner who, as a homeless man in the early 1980s, struggled to maintain his toddler son and worked his way up to finally become CEO of his own stockbrokerage firm. In the film, his son says he is not happy with the grim situation they are in. But, his father, kneels down to the boys level, looks him straight in the eye and says, "No matter what, it is still possible for you to just choose to be happy." The young lad thinks about this for a second and then says, okay dad, I will be happy.

Real happiness is not sought, because it is not outside of us. It is within us.

We do not need reasons to be happy because we can decide to **JUST BE**, just be happy.

When you choose happiness, things change for the better

Record the following prose together with some meditative music. When you have a quiet moment play it back and let the power of the words help lift your mood and settle yourself into a happy frame of mind. This is the gift of happiness:

On choosing happiness

Happiness is a journey without distance.
All thoughts of fear and lack are reversed
the moment we accept that every piece of universal
joy rests already in our hearts.
Whatever we want is here within us, right now.
Wisdom, peace, inspiration is within us.
It is our unconditional selves.
Whatever joy we hoped to get after
we found our true partner,
got the dream job,
bought the ideal home and
earned the right money
is already within us!
To be healed we need to
stop resisting our unconditional self and

make ourselves wholly available
to what is already inside us.
We are inspiration packed, wisdom infused,
made with love and
blessed with joy.
We are everything that we seek.

'**Happiness is inherent in you, and you can have happiness now.**'

The lessons here are:

- The longer you dwell on what has gone wrong, the longer you will go round in circles.
- When you choose to be happy you attract life's best things.

Here are four affirmations you can make:

1. *I am happy.*
2. *I am always looking for the good in myself, others, and the world.*
3. *I am responsible for my own happiness; it is not the job of others.*
4. *I decide to focus on what's right, instead of what's wrong.*

Your plan: In the space below, make a note of what you can do to be in touch with your inherent happiness, even when things are getting tough or going wrong.

....
....
....
....
....
....

3. Practice appreciation

On one of my courses a student told me about how grateful she felt about the things in her life. She mentioned her home, her husband and being thankful for her job. Particularly I recall her telling me how she sits by her daughter's bed when she has fallen asleep and gazes upon her, thinking how wonderful she is, and how lucky she is to have such a wonderful daughter.

Another one of my students sent me a Christmas card. It said, *"I can honestly say I'm a different person. I find good things in each and every day and count myself lucky for all the things I have ... a wonderful husband, nice home, great parents and good friends. And, as for placing my attention on appreciating things, I think the more practice you have, the easier it becomes. The world just seems a better place."*

Appreciation sees past fear

Appreciation is a sincere expression of love, and love is the highest feeling we have. At the other extreme is our most primordial feeling, that of fear. It is a fact that during the times *when we engage with appreciation, we see beyond fear.* Many people throw aside any fears and act in a brave way, or even lay down their lives in order to protect and preserve what they appreciate and cherish.

'Like light dispels darkness, appreciation dispels fear.'

Appreciate life and people

There is plenty of evidence to show that of *all the people in rehabilitation units, and people who are recovering from heart attacks, the ones that get better quicker are the ones who appreciate and love life more.*

'Positive thoughts heal the body. Happy people really do live longer!'

When you show appreciation towards people and things in your life, you will always receive a favourable response from them. On the other hand, if you project dislike, and are a harsh and judging person, then you will give yourself a tense and bitter existence. What goes around comes round. Know that feelings of appreciation and gratitude are healing, because of the benevolent, calming feelings they engender.

Life is good and being good to others makes it so

Life can be a bit like people standing in line to buy a lottery ticket. The people in the queue want something nice to happen in their lives, and one way might be if they won the lottery. The important thing here is that we could split the people in the queue into two different types.

One set of people in the queue are making the best of their time. They take a pleasant interest in things around them and chat to each other. They are content in that moment. Above the sun is shining. It is a clear bright day and the birds are singing. It is one of those days when you feel good to be alive and in the company of other people.

The other set of people, whilst waiting, are not communicating to each other. If they do speak, they are complaining about everything under the sun, except there is no sun for them. As you can expect, the weather is miserable. There are heavy black clouds above; it is incessantly raining, together with flashes of thunder and lightning. The scene is totally grim.

We need to ask ourselves the question, which queue in life would we rather be in? Which queue do we usually find ourselves standing in? Do we want to go through life bickering and complaining, and never wanting to see the beauty that is all around? There is an old saying: *"Who is right, the pessimist or the optimist? Well, both are right!"* There is more than one way of looking at something. It depends upon one's point of view as to what is right or wrong, and we are all entitled to our belief systems. So, **why be negative when you can just as easily change your view to one that is more positive? The rewards are worth the change of mind. You will live longer, and feel better, so why not give it a whirl?**

Be mindful of your appreciation

A way of becoming happier and receiving more from life is, each day, to practice being mindful of your appreciation of things. For example, take time out to think of the positive things that your friends, or loved ones, or parents, have done for you. Observe your feelings during this time. Don't be surprised if your mood lifts and you feel energised.

One person I know, who lives on her own, said that before she entered her flat she thought about the goodness of the people who live next to her. Subsequently, she reported increased contact with them and experienced the friendliness that she sought.

What are the little things that you appreciate?

Think about the events of your day and look for the little treasures that stand out. Do you notice, when you shift your focus on to the small things, you start to see the real beauty that surrounds you? It is also heartening to know that what you focus on multiplies, and so the effect on you is an ever increasing spiral of happiness.

'The gift of appreciation and perception of real life comes to those who are mindful of the small things in life.'

Be mindful of your body

Numerous recent clinical studies, which make use of MRI scans and biometric feedback, have shown that being mindful of one's body shows helpful changes in brain structure and chemistry, and raises the spirits of people who suffer with depression, and chronic unhappiness.

Don't detest your body

There may be times when you can be fed up with your body's health, how it looks and so on. This can cause you to hate it, or ignore it. The opposite to this; embracing your body, warts and all, is what will make you and your body live in better harmony. For example, would you run away from a friend who is in trouble? No! You would embrace your friend, offer understanding, your presence, and love. Essentially, it is best to get in touch with your body, not do the opposite of pushing it away. It is a part of you, so don't fight with it. If this happens your mind and body are divided against each other, and this leads to illness.

Appreciate your body

This is about taking your focus off any aspects of your body that are negative, like hating it, feeling detached and not tuned into it. Start by acknowledging that your body is there. Be mindful of what your body does do for you, how wonderful your body is, and how much you appreciate it. It is about relating to your body lovingly, and being considerate to it.

Tune into your body

Tuning into your body is a good start to taking notice of it in a good way. You can do this through a body scan meditation, which I will show you how to do below. In this way you will be noticing your body, thinking how good it is, and sensing its aliveness, its feeling, and its energy.

A meditation for your body

Sit or lie down. This is your time out, nothing to do, nowhere to go just for you to simply relax. Lightly close your eyes and focus on your breathing. Get in touch with the movement of your breathing. When you are ready bring your attention to your body. For whatever reason you may not be too happy with your body and, if this is the case, your body knows it. In a way it is a bit like this. Imagine how you would feel if someone followed you around all day telling you that you are not up to much. Even if there is a little truth in this, it can all be reversed for the purpose of improving the vibrancy of energy in your body and in turn your wellness. You start this process with the awareness that, no matter what, your body is always there with you doing its best.

Just think about how great your body really is, because of the millions of processes that are being carried out on your behalf, in billions of cells every second. Always your body is there, asking for little reward in return. And, even though it has faults, or is wearing out, or there are times when you get upset with how it works, or how it looks in the mirror, it still can be appreciated, just as you would appreciate a good friend, or someone who you love who had these shortcomings. As such, when there is trouble with your body don't turn away or run away from it. Instead, as you would treat a friend, or someone who is most close to you, embrace your body and be caring to it. In this way you know your body responds well to the provision of a decent diet, exercise, rest and a regular daily routine.

Knowing it is important to let your body know it is appreciated is a bit like not ignoring a good friend, but instead making them aware you know they are there and that you appreciate them. This can be summed up as mindful awareness of your body – being aware that you are aware of your body. You do this by feeling your body's presence, feeling your body's feelings. In this way, your body and mind become at one with each other. They are not in disagreement but in harmony and this is a sound foundation for your well-being.

Now go back to movement of your breath and when you are ready, bring your awareness to the physical sensation in your body. You can start this awareness of the body by sensing how your toes feel. Feel the energy there, any sensations there. Now bring your awareness to the soles of your feet, and your heels. Let this awareness carry onto your ankles, your calves, your shins, knees and up through your thighs, your groin, genitals, pelvis, buttocks, hips, your lower back, and abdomen, your upper back, chest and shoulders. Then move on to your hands. First with the sensations in your fingers and thumbs, the palms of your hands, the back of your hands, your wrists, lower arms and elbows, your upper arms, your shoulders again and your armpits. Next bring your attention to feeling your face, - the jaw, mouth, lips, nose, cheeks, ears, eyes and forehead and then your whole head.

As you breathe in, become aware of any particular tensions or sensations that come up. Sense what is happening there and release as you breathe out.

Just spend a few moments being aware of the sensations, of the energy, in the whole of your body and of your breath flowing freely in and out of your body.

In your own time you can now come back fully to the room, stretch and wiggle your fingers and your toes. Open your eyes, feel fully refreshed and happy and more positive about yourself and who you are.

Marinade yourself in appreciation before you sleep

If you want to induce feelings of being gratified, as well as ensure sweet dreams, make use of this appreciation technique before you go to sleep.

An appreciation meditation

Sit or lie comfortably, close your eyes, and take a few deep breaths, more slowly than you normally would. Take a moment now to allow the whole of your body to settle, to be still, and to become completely comfortable. Allow your face and jaw and neck to relax. Moving down now, through the rest of your body, let all the muscles just relax. That's right, everything so, easy. Again, become aware of your breathing and allow it to be easy, effortless and natural. Think of those truly wonderful moments in your life when you were cared for, or when you achieved things. Or think of those people that have helped you, or perhaps a person who you love, who makes you laugh, or who inspires you to live. Think also of the dark times you have had, and the valuable lessons this has taught you. Give thanks for all these things that have come into your life, knowing they are gifts.

Be proud of your innocence, your fearlessness, your freedom.

Be thankful for the knowledge that joy rests already in your heart, and that wisdom, peace and inspiration is within you.

Know that you are everything that you seek.

Sit quietly in the thankfulness of your creation and that you are here on earth to live fully and give fully – not just things, but who you are. You are the gift.

Know that love is already yours, as happiness is already yours.

Be proud about the times you coped when life was difficult.

Think about those things that you are good at and like doing, and the good things that you have learned about yourself.

Bring to mind those that have helped you, or befriended you, when times were difficult.

Know the entire universe is here to support you, to open up to life and let people in.

Be reassured that you are loved and safe.

Reflect on the wonderful feeling of love, and receiving from those who are pleased to give to you.

Think of the times when you have been blessed with kindness, intimacy, enjoyment, and nice people.

Cast your mind to the wonder of romance, flowers, sunlit days, and laughter.

Reflect on your appreciation of the truth, trust, and innocence.

Know that at any time you can move towards all this through slowing down, and remember the valuable gift life has given to you; that of being, and being able to take part in life.

Know that you can make your positive choices and take part in life's treasures. Such treasures as, talking to others, helping others, listening, joining in, and having fun.

Sit in silence and spend a moment reflecting on something that you deeply appreciate.

Be thankful for the wisdom that you now feel has entered you.

You can now come back fully to the room. Stretch; open your eyes, and feel fully refreshed, happy, and more positive about yourself and who you are.

The lessons here are:

- Mindfulness around what you appreciate in life promotes happiness and healing.
- Showing appreciation towards others enhances all your relationships.
- When appreciation is present, fear is absent.

Here are four affirmations you can make:

1. *I am appreciative of all the wonderful things in this world, starting with myself and others.*
2. *I am everything I need, and I appreciate that.*
3. *I am mindful of the little things in life, the difficulties, the wonders, the bad, and the good that is in everything. They all help me to be what I am.*
4. *I am appreciative of life itself, and this contributes to my health and happiness.*

4. Chill and enjoy life

We can all get caught up with trying to keep pace with what modern society demands. If we become too driven, this can sometimes bring burnout instead of happiness. Your body, in its wisdom, will send you messages that you are overdoing it. Stop before it shuts you down.

Sometimes we need to stop trying so hard. Has it ever occurred to you that with a 'no pain, no gain' attitude you are trying too hard to be happy? Often we can find that there are areas of our life where we are putting in the most effort, yet nothing seems to work. The fact is, when you are on your game, doing stuff can seem so easy. When the opposite is true, and you are really trying and getting nowhere, this is a sign that there is a better way.

Every business has had more than its share of managers and executives who pushed themselves to the limits each day, never thinking that it would be their body that would turn around and manage them by shutting them down and saying, "Enough is enough." Many senior executives work so hard, they earn themselves a position in a cardiac unit. The lucky ones are those who have a mild heart attack, and learn from the warning. It is these people who realise they need to back off. They may even think they need some kind of psychotherapy to wean them off their work holism. **These people don't need a vocation, they need a vacation.** It is useful to know that:

> *'The greatest form of psychotherapy is relaxation and having your space.'*

Be kinder to yourself

In holding a new-born baby, you would take care, simply because you know you hold a precious and wonderful thing in your arms. And, the truth is, you are just as important; so you need to take care to treat yourself with love and kindness. So, think about when you have done something nice for others, in order to bring them enjoyment. Then remember the old saying, "charity begins at home", and make a start at making yourself happy. If you can't make yourself happy, you will have little chance of making anyone else happy. This being the case, it becomes a given to be more loving and kinder to yourself.

Realise the wonderful fun ways of rediscovering your happiness

Treats are the things that can make life move from dreary to cheerful. For example, treating yourself to visit a good coffee shop to have a delicious cheesecake and a cup of great coffee, or a trip to a health parlour to have a massage. So, what rings your bell? As the Hot Chocolate record goes:

'Are you getting enough of what makes you happy?'

'When you are happy the world is happy with you.'

The wise know that the real lasting pleasures are not to be had from expensive, or exciting, or glittery things. Often, it is the simple, free things in life that make us happy. For me it is getting close to nature, taking in some beautiful scenery and - breathing-in crisp, clean air. What does it for you - going out on brilliant sunlit day, looking at the stars, being near the ocean? When did you last just feel fantastic at just being alive, just to be in this wonderful world? When you are like this, you appreciate life, and never take things for granted. The terminally ill don't. Those who have visited a hospice for the first time get a big surprise. Instead of seeing a grim place where people go to die, they find instead a place which is warm and most positive. They are like this because the people there know the value of life. They don't wait until tomorrow to appreciate things. They appreciate what they have now! When we take a leaf out of their book we start to realise the preciousness of life can always be embraced now, in this moment. And, this moment is always there for all of us.

Get to know how you can practice being kinder to yourself

Take a few moments to just sit back, relax, and think about two or three things you can do in your life, starting today, where you can practice being kinder to yourself. If you want, write them down in the space below.

....
....
....

....
....
....
....
....

The lessons here are:

- When you stop dashing around, become quiet, and take time to just be, more things of value will come into your life.
- When you are kinder to yourself, life becomes kinder to you.

Here are two affirmations you can make:

1. *I am at my best when I resist ego's dash for stuff, and go at my wisdoms pace.*
2. *I am cherished and endowed with love.*

5. Be authentic

I watched a TV programme about magic in which the British magician Paul Daniels tried his hand at putting on a magic show in America. It went reasonably well and he pulled in a small, but enthusiastic, audience. The show then focused on looking at other names in America, who are big on the comedy circuit, like David Copperfield and Penn & Teller. What struck me was how much bigger and more glittery these other professionals, and their acts, looked.

At one point the interviewer remarked to Paul Daniels, *"Don't you feel somewhat inferior now to these slick modern acts?"*

Paul Daniels, who had been doing this type of stuff when these performers were still up and coming, gave the interviewer a wry smile and said,

"Look, I do this because it's what I'm good at, and it's what I like doing. I might not be in the limelight now, and I might not have the big deal acts these others have, with viewing audiences of thousands, but it's what I do, so I do it."

Good for him! I thought. How many of us can say that we do what we like doing? We often do what others want us to do, or we do things that we don't like doing in order not to have such a small act. Small act or not, having your own act is the biggest and best thing that anyone can do.

It's good when we are happy with what we do

My central heating boiler broke down and I rang the appliance company to get it fixed. The repair man they sent seemed very efficient and soon got the problem sorted. One thing I noticed about the chap was that whilst he was working he was singing and humming away to himself. He seemed to be a very happy person. I mentioned this to him and he said. *"Yes, I suppose I am happy. You see, I've been doing this job now for nearly forty years. I enjoy doing this type of work. I suppose it's what I've always wanted to do since being a young lad."*

"There we are, I thought, the same job, all that time. Yet he is happy, he likes what he is doing and has always wanted to do it. He is so lucky, and the brilliant thing is, he knows it too."

This chap did not have what most would think was an adventurous, or glamorous, or uniquely different job. He was not a rocket scientist, or a brain surgeon, or an explorer. He was just a straightforward tradesman. Yet, in my opinion, he had the best job ever, because he had cracked the secret of being happy in what he did. But, even if our job is not the best fit for us, we have cracked it when we can still find ways to be happy in that job.

Don't become part of the wish brigade

Whilst we can seek to be authentic regarding the work we do, we can seek to be authentic regarding living the life that is right for us. It is our birth right to live our best life, one that fulfils us, inspires us and brings us joy.

Don't become one of the I wish brigade … I wish I had done that when I had the chance … I wish I'd have followed my dream … I wish things could have been different … and so on. Don't ever think it's too late! It's never too late, when you can, starting today, invite into your life new and stimulating ways to live.

Know what things are important to you

In one of the spoof alien films that I saw recently there was a poor astronaut whose body was inhabited by a small alien frog like creature. It was inside his leg, and could be seen moving around. The astronaut was terrified what it might do to him. The doctor on the space ship said that the only way out was to amputate his leg in order to get rid of the creature. The astronaut said, "No way are you cutting off my leg." With that, the bug type creature in his leg started to move upwards in the direction of his crutch. He screamed out loud, "Cut it off, cut it off!"

This film sequence was intended to make the audience laugh. I certainly did since the joke was about us, as humans, realising that, *some things are important, but some things are really important!* This can be a timely reminder that we can sometimes forget what is really important in our life. Things like taking time to smell the roses, relationships, our health, our homes, and friendships.

Know what you like doing

Ask yourself: *What is it that makes time fly when you do it? What captivates your imagination so much that you feel totally immersed and fulfilled when you are engaged with it? What would you do for no reward?* All these questions are a strong indicator of what you should be doing more of in your life. If you are already doing these, then you are both wise and lucky. Your rewards are that you will be living an inspired life. For you boredom will not exist, and, because you are making more effective use of your time, your success is inevitable. In fact your wellbeing is always guaranteed when you reshape your life to live a life that is more you.

Often the pressures of work, and life, channel us in the wrong direction and we lose sight of who we are. The following six processes are designed to assist you to rediscover the real you.

1. Write a list of things that you are good at, or that you keep being drawn to.
2. Write down a few top qualities that you love about yourself, or that others have seen in you.
3. What are you looking for? What would make you happy? What do you want and need? What would make a positive difference to your life?
4. What qualities do you want to enhance in your life? For instance, do you want to be more confident, joyful, dependable, friendly, have more fun?
5. What do you want? Ask yourself, "Why do I want it?"
6. What have you attracted or created in your life that you want to change? For instance, perhaps you have to little money, an unsatisfactory partner, a boring job?

Lesson: It's not about what you do, but about who you are. It is your willingness to face the truth about yourself and being authentic that could make difference to you having a meaningful life. Try to live from your core and your spirit, instead of doing something because someone else might like it, or you think you have to.

Talk it over with a friend

Talk to someone you can trust to help to clarify and crystallise your thoughts. Also, listen to them. Ask your friend to talk to you about what they want from life, what they want to achieve, and what their dreams or hopes are. Ask them what they think it will be like when they have achieved their dreams. Having listened to your friend, now talk about your life and plans. If you can, it will help to spend further time reviewing what has been said.

What stops us breaking free?

The reasons people get stuck in poor lifestyles and unrewarding jobs are as varied as there are people. Fundamental to this malaise is the negative picture they have in their mind of their poor chances of success, and feeling that the ties with the present situation are too strong to break. If you are in this trap, there are ways to break free. It is about seeing that what you think might be blocks, are just thoughts. For example:

Fear. Why should fear stop you, it is only a thought. If you don't try, you will miss the opportunity of having a go. If what you do works then you will feel good. If it doesn't, then at least you will have had a go, and will have learnt more about how to handle life.

Opinions of others. Ask yourself, "Am I going to live my life according to what others think, or what I think?" Listening to what others would do is practical, you might learn something, but you know your life is unique, and nobody can feel how you do about things. Therefore, when you take your life decisions in your own hands you not only empower yourself, which will feel good, you are doing what is right for you. So, listen to your own inner guide and reap the benefits of being your own person. You can be a good advisor, since you know yourself better than anyone.

Insecurity. If you don't do what inspires you, you might as well have nothing. Many people tread the treadmill of life in order to reap the security the treadmill offers. They swap authenticity for security. What they get from such a lifestyle is regular and timetabled goodies to keep them going; a bit like being a hamster on its treadmill. It's not a bad life; you get fed regularly, and petted every now and then if you're lucky. But what a life! Is the security of the mundane and basic provisions, a life that a spirited human should be living? Free yourself from any cage you feel you might inhabit because of security. Seek a life of freedom where you call the shots. When you do this you will not only create your own security, you will feel better, and happier than you have ever been before.

Criticism. Criticism can kill, and has done. Remember, if you were perfect you wouldn't be here. It is human to err. Criticism is okay when it is backed up with useful tips on how to do things better. Often it is presented by people with low self-esteem who think they can get over their own faults by pointing out the faults in others. In being authentic you will be able to recognise these types. You will also know there is no need to get angry with them. It is they who are faulty, and all you can do is feel some compassion for their plight.

The desire to be the best. If you follow this desire you might get depressed if you think you have blown it. Fame, and being the best, depends upon the fickle viewpoint of others. Your measure of success should be how well you honour what being you means. This is about you feeling good about yourself on the inside, and, when you do, your life on the outside will feel good also. All you have to do is do the best you can. And, when you are being authentic, you have no need to worry about doing your personal best, because you will already be doing it by being authentic?

Lack of confidence. Life's experience can provide you with a picture of yourself as not being as good, or not doing as well as others. When you feel this way, you have fallen into the comparison trap.

Ultimately this is deadly, with the first casualty being your confidence. Once in this trap you can start to think you are not much use. You can become blind to your worth, and lose confidence in your abilities. Since lack of confidence breeds poor performance, this can act as a self-fulfilling prophesy. And, this is the way you will play out the law of attraction which says, "What you see is what you get." Having a poor me attitude, will always give a poor life. There will always be reasons as to why your situation is different from others, but if you think you are worse off, you can negatively hypnotise yourself to feel you are not up to doing well. And, if you really believe you have a low self-image, this will not help you to see who you really are. If you really knew how wonderful you are, there would be no stopping you.

No longer do you have to let your confidence be sapped by thoughts which are not true. Any perceived barrier will disappear when you experience the confidence of living from the authentic you. The authentic you sees challenges not as threats, but as opportunities to keep trying, and learning. Your authentic you is confident because it is on real purpose, and, as such, is aligned with the power of your Spirits intention, which is for you to be your authentic self in this world.

Money, power, possessions. Your ego thinks it needs these things to make you feel safe and appear good. But, the irony is, instead of freeing you, their pursuit will always keep you tied down. This is because, when you are in a state of wanting, always needing more, this is the life you will lead; one of 'always wanting'. In being authentic your true self is in charge, not your ego. When you seek authenticity, rather than stuff, you will be provided with what you truly are, rather than attempting to acquire what you feel is missing. This way you will live a genuine life, where the rewards are priceless. Priceless because you call the shots, you feel real every day, and your behaviour always validates your worthiness.

Being stuck looking backwards at the past. Your personality, or ego, cannot help but worry about its lack of authenticity. As a cover up, it wishes to blame you, or others, for any mistakes it thinks were made in the past. Chewing over who is to blame can only immobilise you. But, memories are always good when you have lived an authentic life. In this way you have not lived by the rules of others, or to look good, or appear right, but to enjoy every moment of feeling free, and pursuing your passion.

The lesson here is:

- You will be a success when you do what you like doing and are best at.

Here is an affirmation you can make:

I am doing what I love and loving what I am doing. Because of this my life is a gift.

6. Get some passion in your life

It's never too late for a life of passion! Your passion can be for adventure, excitement, joy, fun, something different, a change from the same old. These are the things we seek when we are looking for freedom and love. This is a far cry from when we are operating from fear, or having to please others, or by doing what has always been done. Can you make a start to move away from these constraints? I hope your answer is, "Yes I can!"

> *'Stop being safe, being always tidy and tiptoeing through life into your coffin.'*

The real you is creative, playful and, if you allowed it to express itself, it would unleash its wonder upon you right now. Is it, therefore, necessary to save your brightness, your liberation, for tomorrow? Sometimes it may be too late. *A by word for a more spirited life is 'carpe diem' – literally, 'enjoy the present' and also colloquially 'seize the day'.* Living in the now is the only key to doing this. Living in the now will guarantee you a more successful future than the one you planned for by being your old self. So, step into a life with more passion by being more present to what matters to you, because you matter. When you are really in the moment you allow yourself to experience the wonder and beauty of life; you are happy. It is that feeling which is there now for the taking.

Examples of happy experiences

Feeling the inner glow and total contentment to be with friends

Getting an obvious enjoyment from lovingly preparing and doing things for others.

Feeling appreciated by others

> Being proud and happy for your friends and loved ones when they feel successful and have achieved things they wanted
>
> Being happy for others when they are enjoying themselves
>
> Feeling love towards those close to you and extending it out to others
>
> Being grateful for the many good things that happen in this world

It's never too late to follow you passion

A friend of mine was made redundant and went on a course to retrain for a different job. As part of the course he undertook a psychometric test which showed he had very high natural skills as a coding expert. Since the cold war is over, and there is probably less demand nowadays for code breakers, I couldn't see where he could put these skills to use, apart from working in a library and coding books into their correct library categories. He confessed that although he had worked all of his life as a chemist, he wished he had pursued this type of work. What a shame he hadn't found this out earlier. But, *better late than never because, it's never too late to follow your passion.*

Find your own strange beauty

If there is something you wish to pursue, don't be put off because you feel you don't do it good enough, or others appear to be better at it than you. If it's what you like doing, just do it. Don't worry about what others might say, or think. Think about L S Lowry, best known for his matchstick men and women, who painted scenes of the industrial towns of the north of England. Some other artists, and people, Lowry knew, looked at his work, which portrayed quite desolate urban landscapes and anonymous figures, and said; "Your figures all look like matchstick men, can't you paint them properly?" Lowry replied, "This is me, this is what I do, I like them, I see a strange beauty in them, and that's what matters." In this sense my message to you is, *do your thing, and find your own strange beauty.*

If you build it, they will come

A television programme called 'Grand Designs' presented the story of a carpenter who got permission to build a house on forest land, mainly from forest and farm material. The programme showed him sleeping rough under tarpaulin, and working in all weathers to get the house completed. Two years later the film crew went back to see how he had faired. They were shown around the spacious and comfortable abode he had built. This time he was not alone, for he now had a wife and a new baby. They all looked so wonderfully happy. Here was a man who had a dream. He built his dream and he was joined by others to live in it. By being passionate about what he wanted, he reaped rewards.

This reminded me of the Film, 'The Field of Dreams'[6], in which Kevin Costner plays an Iowa farmer who, despite his family's struggle to hold onto their farm, starts ploughing his corn to build the field. He does so because he hears a voice in the field telling him, "If you build it, he will come." 'It' turns out to be a baseball field, and 'he' is Shoeless Joe Jackson, who was kicked out of baseball almost seventy years before. This incredible film is about more than baseball. It is about second chances, values, heroism, helping right past wrongs. It is about believing and passion for something. The plotline is played off in a terrific scene near the film's end where, from all around the area, the roads are jam packed with people traveling to see the field.

After the film was completed, the real farmer who owned the land started to plough up the field in order to grow corn again. The local farmers asked him not to, saying they would make his money up, if, in return, the field could be left as it was in order that they might all enjoy their particular field of dreams. In line with the spirit of the film, I hope this conveys to you:

'Don't let anybody plough under your field of dreams.'

In Carol Adrienne's book, The Purpose of Your Life[7], following your passion is summed up beautifully in the following way:

'You will really know when you are doing your life purpose. When you can't see the light [or the purpose], you go out and do what makes you happy. You won't be good for anybody anyway if you

don't make yourself happy. Follow the passion, this is your highest state of existence.'

Do you want passion or contentment?

In the film 'Serendipity' a couple, Jonathan and Sara, played by John Cusack and Kate Beckinsale, briefly meet one night in New York and realise they are meant for each other. As a test of their love they decide to go their separate ways and see if their love would reunite them. They lose touch and, although they both desperately want to get together again, life gets in the way of them finding each other.

Ten years later they are each set to marry someone else, but, before they go through with their respective weddings, Jonathan and Sara seek one last chance to see if their love was real. Jonathan co-opts his best friend, who is an obituary column writer for the New York Times, into helping him find his lost love. The friend, begrudgingly at first, provides help, and in doing so realises that his friend is really intent on changing his life to follow his passion of finding his love, Sarah. Realising that Jonathan has, in effect, dropped his old life to pursue his passion, he writes his obituary and gives him it to read. He reads it out aloud so that we, the audience, can hear it. It goes along the lines that his friend, who was a good chap and was liked by everybody, had now died. He had died to become a new person. A new person who, in order to seek his lost love, was willing to take risks, even appear stupid, and sometimes not always fit in with everyone's expectations. As a last throw of the dice, Jonathan and Sara, go to the place where they first met. Since they each did this without the others knowledge, they hope against hope that they can bump into each other again. They each get there, but still miss each other. Each thinks they have failed, and each sits dejected. Then, at the last minute, they see each other and come together realising that their love for each other is still there, and now they are reunited at last.

You know that to change in such a way can take great courage, since often it seems better to stay put when things appear to be reasonably okay. *In other words, you can settle for comfortable. But, in doing so, you can become unconscious to the realness that living a real and true life can offer you.*

What could you say about your life?

Earlier civilisations did not write obituaries because they thought them to be a waste of time. All they wanted to know about a person was, did they have passion in their life?

Write your own obituary, as if you had died now. What could you say about yourself? *Have you died to the humdrum of settling for a life that is agreeable, or are you living a life that has passion?*

Think from the end and just do it

Often you may be discouraged from doing things because you may not be sure about the details of how to do it. Such a worry can stop you from starting things. Have faith you will be helped, but make sure you try to do what you can. *It is important to have a go by finding out what needs to be done and start doing it. As the Nike advert says: "Just do it."* Your main job is to think from the end. That is, imagine how your intention will be achieved, and do not dwell on how obstacles may block your path. Deal with the problems as they arise, and have faith in your wisdom and strength. Also, ask for help, and give thanks for the help that will come. *It is important to know if you get lost, you will be shown the way to do it.* Remember, Spirit is the unseen force which can assist you in the accomplishment of your tasks. Ask for help, it will come. It will.

Knowing that this help, whatever form it may take, is there, will give you strength since it means you do not have to travel on your quest alone. It is like being on a journey and knowing there is someone, or something, most powerful by your side.

Establish a daily intention

What you now need to do each day is ask yourself:

- What is required of me? In other words, get your priorities right in terms of what you must do to be a better partner, work colleague, friend, daughter, son, husband, wife, parent, etc.
- What makes me fulfilled? You can hurry around and get a lot of things done, but you may not be fulfilled. However, make sure

you have dealt with the requirement question above, before you start with the fulfilment question. By arranging your priorities this way, your chances of making a positive transformation are increased dramatically. If you hold these two questions uppermost in your mind you will attain true fulfilment.

- Don't make the mistake of coming to the end of your life and discovering that you have not lived your dream. The purpose of your life is to get your dream established in your mind, and then do something about it. Remember, it is your dream and not someone else's. Make it happen! Create your own dreams and live life to the fullest.

Be persistent

The mantra for achieving success in life is to keep trying. Be persistent. Never give up. The world is full of people with qualifications, and talent, who have failed. Even genius will fail without determination. A nice little saying sums this up: "A big shot is little shot that kept shooting." The nice feeling behind this saying is, *by doing something you satisfy yourself that you did have a go. If you didn't have as go, you will never know. This is why persistence always pays off.* This leads me to another saying, *'Keep on, it's not over until the fat lady sings.'*

Never Give Up

Winston Churchill was invited back to Harrow School to give the end of year speech to the boys. As their most famous living 'old boy', they completely ignored the fact that he'd hated it there, and had left with the admonition ringing in his ears from his Masters that he'd never amount to anything.

When the great day arrived the boys sat in nervous expectancy, waiting to hear from this famous orator. He stood, looked out over the audience of eager young faces and barked,

"Never give up!" followed by a pause.

"Never give up!" another pause.

"Never give up!" And he sat back down again.

His striving, and subsequent achievements, as well as yours, can be summed up by that mantra?

The lesson here is:
- Allowing your passion for life to expresses itself stimulates your being, maintains your aliveness, and keeps you happy.

Here are two affirmations you can make:
1. *I am life itself, totally involved with life.*
2. *I am creative, playful, living in the now; awake to the wonder and beauty of life.*

7. Have more fun!

When I was a University academic, one of the modules I ran was for the students to learn to develop and run a real small business. The students were split into teams and tasked to develop a business plan and then run a viable company. The student teams were assessed through having to make a presentation about how well they had achieved this.

On their assessment day I listened to each team's presentations. Each had been good, but when the last team had presented, what they said really made me think. They reported they had done this and that, and had learnt a lot, but they admitted that there was one important thing that they had got wrong.

"How honest they are", I thought, "But what was it?"

The reply came, "We didn't have fun and if you don't have fun in business, even if you are successful and can make money, then in the final analysis you have missed out, and your life has been the poorer from it. We now realise that it would have been better if we had gone and set up a business in which we could enjoy things and have had some fun."

As a tutor, I knew the other students present could not have been given a better lesson concerning what really matters when we journey along the road of our careers and life. So, be enterprising, have fun!

Are you having a full pie or just left with the crumbs?

When I was at work there was an administrator I knew whose list of duties and responsibilities seemed to be endless. She usually worked late but one day she said to me, "I'm leaving early today. My husband's getting a bit fed up with me living at this place, so I'm going home to be wifey to him." I laughed inside and the next day we both talked about how much of our lives are given up to others, or to other things.

In a way each of our lives is like a pie. A bit of the pie is given up to being a husband, or a wife, or a brother, sister, friend, lover, relative, and so on. When the different pieces of the pie have been taken up, is there any left for yourself, or is there just the crumbs?

We need to start dealing with each other as real people, each with our own needs and interests. Initially it is difficult because we can forget who we were as people. So often we get busy with life and, bit by bit, we lose touch with the essence of who we are. Before the pieces of the pie are taken up we need to look at what piece we are, otherwise we will be left just picking up the crumbs.

If you are that pie, then you need to ask the question, "What piece is left for me after all the others have taken their share?" At the end of life, some people don't even know what kind of pie they were. Know what kind of pie you are. Live this life, and leave this life, knowing who you are.

Questions: What kind of pie are you, what are the pieces? If you wish to change things, what kind of pieces would be in your pie?

Focus on a real life not the chores

My wife often tells me I am lazy because I don't do enough repairs around the house and such like. I tell her, she is so lucky to have me because how many wives get taken to a café nearly every day, how many wives get flowers weekly, how many wives get taken on a ramble as soon as the weather is nice, and so on.

My view is that the housework will be there when we are not. Of course basic things need to be done, but the priority should be on getting them out of the way to lead a real life. **At the end of my life I am not going to slip away knowing I have not lived it to the full.** Life is to be lived, and to be lived with others, Get out, meet others, and live life to the full. Life is about your well-being and being well to others. It is about relationships. Make a start on this by respecting your right to a fun filled authentic life, thereby giving yourself the best relationship with yourself you could ever have

Don't be too logical - see what matters in life

Think about the words in 'The Logical Song', by Supertramp. *"When I was young, it seemed that life was so wonderful, a miracle, oh it was beautiful, magical.*

.... But then they send me away to teach me how to be sensible, logical, responsible, practical. And they showed me a world where I could be so dependable, clinical, intellectual, cynical.... Won't you please, please tell me what we've learned I know it sounds absurd but please tell me who I am."

Imagine an intellectually correct world. Here logic, not emotion, might rule. Everything would have to be precise, leaving little room for error. It all seems a bit cold and joyless. Human expression like warmth, comfort, hope and wonder, might seem too whimsical. In such a world surprises would seem wrong and different views, if not backed up by knowledge, would be discouraged. This would all go against our humanness, our ability to take wrong turns, for whatever reason, and stumble into new territory. When we veer off the logical fast lane of life we give ourselves the chance to slow down and see things better. If we are lucky we might catch sight of who we really are.

'We can be too logical to see our own reality.'

Make room for fun

On reaching the age of seventy a friend of mine became very poorly with leukaemia, another went nearly blind. Both left very secure jobs in order to retire early in their mid-fifty's. Many of their colleagues said they were silly going so early, and that they would financially regret their decisions. Since then, each has said to me it was the best decision they ever made, since they have had many more years available in which they were free to do what they wanted. Our life is precious and, even if there is no option than to continue working, we should all make a start now on making room for fun and putting some joy into our lives.

You can't buy time!

On day, I got talking to an old chap I knew, and I asked him what he thought about stepping out of the rat race for a while, even if it only to draw breath. I will never forget what he said. "Those who take time out get everything. Remember, you can't buy time!"

Why not trip over joy

Sometimes we need to let go and go with the flow of life. We need to stop any frantic seriousness and take time out to bring some joy into our life. Some of the words from Hafiz's poem, 'Tripping Over Joy'[8], pictures this brilliantly:

The saint knows
That the spiritual path
Is a sublime chess game with God
And that the Beloved
Has just made a Fantastic Move
… Whereas, my dear,
I am afraid you still think
You have a thousand serious moves.

Being serious is the opposite of letting go. In letting go we should not feel it is necessary for us to be in control, in order for everything to be okay. Things work out right when we take ourselves less seriously, and remember to be joyful, because there is something that creates galaxies and life that has always been moving things in our favour.

Finding yourself

Where in your life do you need to slow down? When you do, you will catch up with yourself and see what really matters. Your new found clarity of thought will free you from the burdens of material correctness many others hamper themselves with.

Slow down, get some peace and remember who you are. The album 'America', has on it a song called 'A Horse With No Name', and a few of the words in the song seem appropriate here:

"I've been through the desert on a horse with no name … In the desert you can remember your name 'cause there ain't no one for to give you no pain … You see I've been through the desert on a horse with no name. It felt good to be out of the rain. In the desert you can remember your name 'cause there ain't no one for to give you no pain."

When you slow down you catch up with what really matters in life.

When you are in *'your natural state'* you are on your game

The ways of being just described were; *life not being a chore, life not being too logical, making room for some fun, having joy in your life and slowing down.* Have you noticed that the more you are in what I would call *'your natural state'*, the more creative and successful you are. This is because in your natural state you are best able to handle things, solve problems, and most capable of making the correct choices. You are really on your game; what athletes call being in the zone.

It is important that you make this connection; *'when you are in your natural state, you are on your game.'*

Being off your game

Have you noticed that when you act from a position of feeling stressed, wound up, angry, and upset, things don't work out that well. This is because, *'when you are in your unnatural state; and you act from it, you are off your game, and will be less successful.'*

A fool proof way to get on your game

None of us want to be like this, but there is a fool proof, straightforward, way to be on your game; simply checkout your feelings. If your emotions are all over the place, and basically you feel upset, stop trying to control things, let go and chill for a while. The time to move ahead, and make choices, is when you feel okay and when problems don't seem to be problems. When you are like this you are relaxed, alert, present, enjoying things, connecting easily with people. In a word, you are in your natural state; in the ways of being described above.

The lessons here are:
- You were put on this earth to be happy; having some fun helps. It helps others too.

- When you are happy, you are in your natural state, and this is when you are on your game.

Here are two affirmations you can make:
1. *I am full of fun. I am up for fun, and spreading fun to others. I do what I like doing and am best at.*
2. *I am creative and successful, this is my natural state.*

8. Be in touch with who you really are

Our life in this world shapes us. We take on a persona and develop a self-image. Other words for this are our conditioned self, our story, ego, and, our personality.

> *'That person, who we think we are, can suffer when it feels it misses the mark in terms of how things with us should be.'*

The result can be low self-image, fear, harmful emotions and bad judgements on ourselves and others. Our suffering can cause us to plough on with more of what our personality thinks should be done to make matters better. If things don't work out, maybe this is the time when we should ask, "What lesson is being given to me here?" One answer is that our learned self can only do so much.

Hopefully we will see the need to shift to doing things based on who we really are.

'Who we really are has unaffected vision, and can see clearly the truth of a situation. This is our true self, our true nature, our essence, our eternal self.'

But, life can make us cynical about that, or we simply don't wish to know. When our consciousness shifts to the degree that we care to connect with our true self, the proof of experiencing happiness will tell us that we did the right thing. The answer to why this happens is that our true self is always about what our personality doesn't think it has; things like freedom, beauty, courage, inspiration, selflessness, compassion, respect, honesty, and love. Often our lives are far from this because we forget who we really are.

Like a good friend, the closer we get to our true self, the more we will feel we belong to it, are part of it, and are embraced by it. Our true self has everything we need in order to be happy and fulfilled. However, it is our conditioned self, which can get in the way of benefiting from what our true self always offers. We can block the good stuff. We do this when we dwell in a lower state of consciousness, brought on by feelings such as, lack, blame, jealousy, hatred, and anger. In this state of unhappiness, the quiet tune of our true self's wisdom is masked by the mind playing its noisy chatter of low level thoughts.

You can help move things along

The good news is that you have the ability to remove any obstacles you may have to your true self's help. It is to do with the higher consciousness of the state of being happy. When you choose to be happy, and are aware of what happiness is, your state of consciousness is raised, and this aligns you more with your true self. In other words, your raised consciousness opens you up to receive more and more of what your true self is always offering. The payoff is, that which seemed to restrict your happiness and fulfilment will just fade away.

Getting closer to your true self

You get closer to your true self by acting, and thinking, in ways that are the closest to what your true self is. And since your true self is pure love, this means being as loving as you can in ways such as forgiving, caring, calming, inspiring, supporting, trusting, and generous. But, like the rest of us, you may feel that life brings you down to the antithesis of these loving ways. Yes, life happens, and when it does it can reduce us to ways that are unforgiving, uncaring, stressed, uninspired, unsupportive, distrusting, and ungenerous. But, the wonderful thing is; this is not what you really are. You are what you came as. You came as your true self, and, as I have said, your true self is love. You are love; this is your unaffected state. So, when life drags you down, as it sometimes does, it is always possible to move up from any low unloving state, to your naturally higher state of love. This is what I mean by raising your consciousness level to align with your true self. Now, this may all appear to be abstract, but it is not. There is a very practical way we can shift our energy upwards; to move from the low feelings life can put us in, to align with the higher energy of our true self. I call this shifting from a low material focus to a true self focus.

Shifting from a low material focus to a true self focus

To shift from a low material focus to a true self focus, it is necessary for you to identify any low unloving states you may have. Let's say these could be anger or hopelessness. Your job now is to contemplate just the opposite of these states, which in this case are peace and hope. This is what will start the shift from a low unloving state, to a higher state of love. In doing this, you are, in effect, shifting from a low material focus to a true self focus. This will happen very quickly, because making the choice between which of these two ways to live is a no brainer. It is only natural to ditch any miserable way of living, in favour of a great way to live. Certainly, once you have tried this for yourself, you will reap the benefits and know that it works.

A true self focus opens you up to everything good

Put another way, a true self focus opens up helpful possibilities, and the payoffs will never diminish. For example, being loving just multiplies its effect. Whereas, a low material focus can, if dwelt upon, give rise to more of the same. Even if the material focus is high, e.g. I have just got this great job, or I have just met this wonderful person who really loves me; please note that things can still turn sour. With a true self focus your underlying okayness is never threatened. Not only are the vagaries of a material focus transcended, but the embodiment of your true self qualities will support you in continually bringing to fruition what will always last. For example, where there may have been fear, there will be love and security. Where there might have been hatred, there will be love and support. Where perhaps there was mistrust, there will be love and respect.

The spur to making the shift, from a low material focus, to a true self focus, is to see that chewing over the ins and outs of any low feelings you may have, like shame, anger, regret, guilt, and fear, is a futile thing to do. You need to simply answer the question, "Do I want to keep stuck like this?" If you don't, it is in your hands to unstick yourself, and move beyond any lowness, since it is unhelpful to you. You do this to give yourself a better life. In deciding to move on, the stuck energy of being upset is released, and you become freer to make useful changes in your life.

Examples of low material focus and true self focus

The left hand column below shows some examples of low material focus, whilst the right hand column shows some examples of true self focus.

Low material focus	True self focus
Grief	Letting go
False self	Becoming authentic
Grievances	Forgiving
Damaged ego	True self
Feeling used / abused	Giving / caring
Shame	Service / helping others

Anger	Peace
Worry	Being in the now
Regret	Being in the now
Guilt	Clear / sane mind
Fear/stress	Love / peace
Fear of shortage	Generous

The first example of a low material focus is, *'grief'*. Its counterpart true self focus is *'letting go'*. Letting go means leaving behind the stuckness of grief, to see helpful possibilities in life. It is possible for you to do this when you identify with the qualities of your true self. When you do this you liberate yourself to live your best life. The following shows you how to do this, and in so doing you will acquire the ability to help others too.

A true self focus through four deeds

A true self focus can be induced through conducting four simple, but profound, deeds:

1. Contemplation - thinking
2. Affirmation – assertion
3. Requesting help - asking
4. Action - doing

If, say, your intention is to adopt a true self focus to overcome grief, the four deeds could be used in the following way:

1. Contemplation

This is the act of focussing your attention on the qualities of your true self which can help shift you from the material focus that is bringing you down. If say you want to shift from the low material focus of grief, then, each day you could contemplate on ways out of your grief. That is, you would sit quietly and let your mind dwell on what it would be like to get over your grief. Think about moving on and being happy. Think about your life now being what you make it, in terms of enjoying things, and being contented. What people, things, and situations, could you use in order to make your world brighter?

2. Affirmation

Here you would affirm that you are the antithesis of a grief full state. That is, you would make affirmations of being happy, glad, enjoying, delighted, elated, joyful, contented, and satisfied. For any of these happy states, visualise where you could be, who you might be with, and what you might be doing. Importantly, to fix any happier state further into your consciousness, summon in yourself the good feelings of what you are visualising.

Here are five affirmations you could make:

1. *I am peaceful now, because the past is let go of and healed.*
2. *I am managing well, because I have learnt from the past and it has strengthened me.*

3. *I am enjoying my life, because I live fully in the present.*
4. *I am satisfied with what I have, because I appreciate life's gifts.*
5. *I am joyful, because I anticipate a future full of helpful possibilities.*

3. Requesting help

Put your faith in your true self helping you overcome your grief. Ask your true self to help you cope and move in ways that will help you. If you have any questions about your grief, stop them churning around in your head by giving the questions over to your true self to help you see the way forward. Know that your true self, in its own time, will come to your help. Be patient. This faith in the power of your true self is really all you need to move on and live a happier life.

4. Action

What actions can you agree with yourself you are going to do this week to move on from any grief you may have? Could it be doing things like: *Making sure you see some friends and acquaintances, and letting them know how much you value them. Getting out and about to enjoy and appreciate what there is. Making plans to go somewhere, or do something you enjoy. Seeing what you can do to bring happiness into someone's life.*

Make a decision to do things like this every week.

Your true self moves you from lowness

In being closer to your true self you get back to the essence of who you really are. This means you move on rather than keeping low. At an instinctual level this is what you are here to do; as well as help others to do the same.

The lessons here are:
- In choosing to be happy, and being aware of what happiness is, your raised state of consciousness aligns you with your true self.
- Your true self's wisdom is always there for you.

Here are two affirmations you can make:
1. *I am aligned with my true self.*
2. *I am powerful, loving, intelligent, and wise.*

9. Imprint the ideas of happiness into your subconscious

What you have looked at, so far, has been ways and means of informing your conscious mind of how you can be happier. Did you know there is another way to raise your level of consciousness of happiness? I hope you are interested, because this way is quite simple, and most powerful. It involves communicating with your subconscious.

Your subconscious works in the background and automatically guides your actions and behaviour. The subconscious is a bit like a sponge which soaks up lessons and principles, and do's and don'ts, which you have noticed since you were born. It enables you to do quite complex things, and make choices, without having to think about them. In effect, your subconscious runs the shop for you. Unfortunately, life being what it is, your subconscious, besides knowing what happiness is, knows a lot about unhappiness. But, it is always possible to loosen attachments to your subconscious beliefs about unhappiness, whilst expanding its knowing of happiness. The means by which this can be achieved is through hypnosis.

I am not about to go into the ins and outs of hypnosis, but, as a hypnotherapist, I know there are straightforward and effective ways of enriching your subconscious awareness of happiness. With this done your life is enhanced because you now, in effect, have a more effective happiness engine running continually on your behalf.

How you input happiness into your subconscious

I will show you how to do this through explaining how you can make use of a *trance state meditation on happiness.* It is a way of quietening your conscious mind, which can be critical and block suggestions, whilst imprinting the ideas of happiness and beingness of happiness into your subconscious mind. Whilst this might sound fancy, the plain fact is, if you practice this trance state meditation you will start to think, see and feel things differently, in a way which is most beneficial to you. And, more and more of your happiness will shine through. This happens because, although your critical mind may, at times, think this happiness stuff is a load of tosh, your subconscious mind just accepts it as useful input. And it is, because happiness is really all about love, and this opens you up to life's possibilities. Whereas, often our conscious mind is driven by various forms of fear and anxiety, and this always holds us back and stops us having genuine relationship with life and people.

How to set things up

To make this work requires you to set aside some time, say ten minutes, in a quiet and comfortable environment, where you will not be disturbed. If you want, you can record this trance state meditation so that you can listen to it. Or, possibly, you can get a friend to speak it out for you. If not, simply relax and read it out to yourself. Before you start this, I suggest you lie down on a carpeted floor with a pillow to support your head. A comfy sofa is also just fine.

I guarantee you will thoroughly enjoy doing this. What's more, if every three weeks you take time out to repeat this trance state meditation, then, over nine weeks, when you will have done it three times in total, you will experience the effects of being happier.

A trance state meditation on happiness

Preparation

Sit comfortably, close your eyes, and take a few deep breaths, more slowly than you normally would. Take a moment now to allow the whole of your body to settle, to be still, and to become completely comfortable. Allow the tension in the muscles of your body to dissipate. Become aware of your breathing, and allow your breathing to be easy, effortless and natural. Simply allow your breath to flow freely and whenever your mind wanders, just bring it back to your breathing, and again allow your breathing to be very easy, effortless and natural.

Now bring your awareness to your body. I want you to think about those little muscles in the skin of your scalp and just allow them to let go and relax ... let your face totally relax, let it soften, let your jaw go slack ... let your whole head just relax ... because the more you physically relax, the more you can mentally relax. Now down to your neck, shoulders, arms and chest, just relax everything ... let yourself unwind ... letting all tensions drain away as you think on down to your tummy, hips, and legs ... right the way down to your feet and toes ... all the muscles of your body beautifully relaxed and easy ... very lazy ... everything nice and relaxed. That's right, everything nice and easy ... so relaxed and safe.

Being happy

Now you can tell yourself; I am happy and know what really matters in life is both being and spreading fulfilment and happiness. When I am happy my brain patterns change, my physiology changes, I think clearer, and make better decisions. Thinking this way releases endorphins and dopamine into my body and this makes me feel good. I sleep better and better sleep produces happiness. When I am truly happy I am radiant and function fully. Above all, I am loving, for the essence of happiness is love. In particular when I am happy, I find that people instinctively gravitate towards me and like me. In being happy I am more independently minded since I own my own emotions.

To maintain my happiness I see any upsetting thoughts for what they are, just thoughts. I choose to be happy, even when situations seem miserable. I look to appreciate things more. I seek to lead a peaceful and enjoyable life. In doing what I like doing and am best at, I will maintain the purpose and passion in my life. Also, I intend to have more fun, and practice being happy, even when things may be difficult.

I have good life enhancing perceptions, attitudes, beliefs, thoughts, and feelings about myself, others, life and the world. My happiness is the power that helps me transcend my problems. When I am happy, when I embrace happiness, I believe in myself! Happiness is in me. I choose this happiness.

My true self

I make it my intention to be fully peaceful, fully relaxed and fully present. Also, my intention is to accept and be open to love, joy, and happiness. I allow myself to smile inside, and if it helps, I picture a moment in time when I remember feeling wholly joyous, completely loved, and at great peace. My whole face feels soft, cool and relaxed, and I remember some great times, or a person perhaps who I love, who makes me laugh, or who inspires me to live. I remind myself that my unconditional self is always there. It is the real me, my true self. It is my innocence, my fearlessness, my freedom. It is my lack of connection to my real self that leads me to participate in illusions of struggle, fear, smallness and unworthiness. Happiness is not in things, it is in me.

Happiness is journey without distance

The fear that something is missing somewhere in my life is a great illusion that creates self-doubt, self-criticism, and self-attack. It brings me that 'not good enough' feeling, a feeling of lack, loss, isolation, neediness, dependency and much pain. This falsely leads me to search somewhere else for happiness. This misperception is what feeds my 'not good enough' feeling. All thoughts of fear and lack are reversed the moment I accept that every piece of universal joy rests already in my heart, the home of my true self. To be healed I need to stop resisting my true self and make myself wholly available to what is already inside me. I know that wisdom, peace, inspiration is within me. I am everything that I seek and know happiness is a journey without distance.

I am everything I need

Healing happens whenever I choose kindness instead of judgement, forgiveness instead of self-attack, laughter instead of condemnation. Life always gets better when I treat myself better. The best act of healing is to accept that there is nothing wrong with me. Who I am, my true self, remains whole, worthy and well. I make a point of looking for the good in everyone I meet. As I offer this light to others so will I strengthen it in myself. I realise the truth about the gift I really am. I forget my self-imposed image, so that my true beauty can shine through. I am open to see the truth of who I really am, i.e. my true self. I am more than the labels I give myself.

I am ready for happiness now, to accept the wonder of who I really am, to be open, to be rid of self-attack. I can see others in this way, and can be there to help and give love. We are all one, and love embraces us.

Completing

It is now time to leave this meditative state, knowing you can come back to it any time you wish. So, make a start of coming back fully into the room by wiggling your hands and toes and having a good stretch.

The lessons here are:

- Hypnosis can be used to loosen attachments to any scepticism around happiness.

- Hypnosis can be used to enhance your subconscious awareness of happiness.

Here are two affirmations you can make:

1. *I attach no importance to any beliefs, conscious, or unconscious, I may have had around being unhappy.*
2. *I am mindful, both in my conscious mind and my subconscious, of what happiness is.*

10. Being happy and practicing happiness

When we are being happy we simultaneously put our happiness into practice in the outside world. In this way our happiness reaches fulfilment because, not only do we have it for ourself, but, we give it to others. Now we have what can be called *'real happiness'*. So, we have *'being happy'* and *'practicing happiness'* which constitute *'real happiness'*. This can be expressed as the happiness equation, which is:

'Being happy and practicing happiness = real happiness.'

Being happy

Being happy is our natural state, and when we are in this happy state of being we naturally create more happiness in the world. This is because of the fundamental law:

'You manifest what you are being'.

The way you are *being* determines what you will experience in your day, your relationships, your job, your travels, where you live; in fact everything in your life. If for example, your state is one of being lonely then you will experience more of the same in your life. Hate begets hate, anger begets anger, low moods beget low moods, and so on. This is simply the law of attraction coming into being. The universe can only match you with the energy you are sending out; since like attracts like.

'The secret behind happiness is, if you want to be happy, be happy!'

Underneath any poo our being is wonderful

At times, things go wrong for us and, when it does, it can feel as if our life has turned to poo. The reality is that everyone, at times, feels like this. It does not mean that life is poo! It just feels like that at the time. Our true self can take a higher perspective and knows that things do blow over, that life can be wonderful, and that we could get on with enjoying other aspects of our life. But, because we have an ego, often, when poo happens, we waste our life energy, metaphorically speaking, painting nail varnish over the poo. We feel we need to spend time on doing this, in terms of things like, trying to look good, needing to win, worrying what others think, judging ourselves as inadequate, being upset when others seem to have more, and so on. All this is stressful and self-defeating. What we forget is that any poo is only temporary and, in reality, is just a thought. Underneath, there is nothing wrong with us. In fact, we really are wonderful.

'When we understand that underneath any poo, we really are wonderful; we will manifest a wonderful life.'

If we don't get this, we could be stuck with low moods. The following explains that low moods give bad solutions, but by being upbeat you will attract useful possibilities into your life.

Low moods give bad solutions

To get us out of any misery we feel, our brains look for solutions. The trouble is, our brain mechanically reacts by bringing its intellectual capability to focus our attention on studying the very things that have made us unhappy. In other words, we attempt to solve the problem at the same level at which it was created. *This is like expecting a disabled person to improve their mobility if they study the causes of arthritis*. We can escape this self-imposed quandary if we stop dwelling on what has gone wrong. Put another way:

'It is possible to become happy directly, without first ascertaining why we have become unhappy.'

The next time you are in a bad situation, remain in the moment with it and feel how you feel. You should never block your emotions. Giving yourself time also allows your mind not to react in haste. Low moods do lead to bad decisions. Such moods do pass, and when they do you are able to see more useful possibilities for your life.

Practicing happiness

In being happy this is the gift you have that you can share with the world. In being happy you are naturally disposed to, and capable of, practicing happiness. And, the more you do, the happier others will become.

'Practicing happiness is a hands-on, alive in the now thing. The more you exercise it the stronger it gets.'

Practice being happy - especially when the going gets tough

It is no good being a fair weather athlete and just training our happiness muscles when things are going fine for us. The best returns are when we practice being happy when things are going wrong. In fact, there is always good in any low state you may experience, since this is being sent as a signal to tell you there is something more about happiness you need to know. Your happiness from this point on will always increase.

Getting on with things versus feeling sorry for myself

Once, just before I was scheduled to give a talk, my wife became very ill and had to be whisked off to hospital. I was told there was nothing that I could do at the moment, and that she was in the hands of experts. Moments later, I found myself sitting on the edge of my bed, head in my hands, bemoaning the situation. "Would my wife be okay, how could I go and talk to people in the state I was in?" were the questions that I asked myself. I caught a reflection of my sad self in the mirror opposite, and saw how pathetic I looked. I realised there was nothing I could do, other than to pick myself up and get on with my life. Feeling sorry for myself, and being incapable of doing things, was not an option I was willing to entertain. It certainly would not help my wife! I knew it was best to keep going and that, one day, my wife would be well. As a result of this experience, I can say:

"The answer to your problems is not to go below the line of neutral human feelings to explore your misery, but to go above it to utilise your strength."

Use it or lose it

Stan had read all the books on how to be happy and he had been in therapy for many years in an attempt to raise himself from his depressed and unhappy view of life. Stan had plenty of stock answers on how to become happy. He could quote chapter and verse what different text books said on the topic, and so often parroted back my teachings. I think he was even more eloquent at expressing them than me. Stan understood what happiness was, and had all the knowledge of how it could be attained. The trouble was that he did not do it. Stan had little time for enjoying himself because he was on intimate terms with his own unhappiness. And, despite advice, all he did was wallow in the gloom of his situation, instead of putting into action ways that he knew could improve matters.

Like Stan, as a result of experiencing our life traumas we, too, can feel defeated and let our thoughts tell us we are a victim of life's circumstances. If we let this happen we are conditioning our self to be continually unhappy. A way out of this is to look at what happiness can tell us to do in this moment. It can tell us that we need to realise the gift we have bestowed on us as a result of experiencing any problem. The gift is that the bad stuff is nudging us to make changes. Also, the gift is being able to put into practice being happy, despite what is happening around us.

'When you really get this, you will experience the true peace of happiness, even when life is difficult. It is like walking in the midst of a great battle where cannons are blasting and soldiers are falling

down mortally wounded; yet, you remain unscathed, because it is not your battle.'

You don't have to be dragged down by any drama. You can choose to rise above it; and know, that despite whatever happens, you are okay. You are now in charge of feeling good about who you are.

'When you put your happiness into practice you have the gift to make others feel good too.'

The lessons here are:
- When happiness is at the forefront of your thoughts, and actions, you will become happier.
- You manifest happiness when you are being happy.
- The way out of misery is not to explore it.
- You cannot solve a problem with any low state of mind that may arise from it.

- If you are unhappy, don't stay with it. The bad feeling you have as a result of being unhappy is really a gift to tell you to put into practice ways you can be happy.

Here are five affirmations you can make:
1. *I am a happy being and therefore I manifest happiness.*
2. *I am a happy being and strengthen my happiness by putting being happy into practice.*
3. *I am not miserable; my real self is just the opposite.*
4. *I am happy, and I do not ruminate on upsets because my energy is directed on being happy.*
5. *I know what happiness is, and any bad feelings I experience reinforces that I need to put being happy into practice.*

A plan for your continued happiness

The ten ways of being happy I have just discussed with you are:

1. *See past your thoughts*
2. *You can choose happiness*
3. *Practice appreciation*
4. *Chill and enjoy life*
5. *Be authentic*
6. *Get some passion in your life*
7. *Have more fun!*
8. *Be in touch with who you really are*
9. *Imprint the ideas of happiness into your subconscious*
10. *Being happy and practicing happiness*

Everything is now in place for you to experience real happiness in your life. This is what I suggest you can now do.

Take a few moments just to sit back, relax. Whilst you are relaxed, consider the above ten ways of being happy, and think about two or three things you can do in your life, starting today, where being happy becomes your focus. I suggest you choose a way of being happy that, at first glance, may be your main sticking point, or seem to be the most difficult for you to do. Tackling this first could make the most inroads to your continuing happiness.

An affirmation

If, for example your first choice of being happy is *'to see past your thoughts'*, here is an affirmation you could use:

"I practice seeing past my thoughts by taking time to relax, becoming calm, and going within. I just simply am. I experience 'beingness' in the here and now. I just go beyond my personality and ask to be in touch with my true self, my essence, my authentic self. I ask my wisdom to speak to me, to show me in what ways the world is a good place, and what good things I can do to bring me cheer, and also help others."

What action could you take?

The space below is there for you to write down how you could go about seeing past your thoughts.

....
....
....
....
....
....
....

Tying things up

The teaching of happiness has endured because it is much more than telling people how to be positive, despite difficult odds. It is about living the most satisfying life you could imagine is possible.

The golden lesson is that you don't have to try and claim this from the world, because you were created with the knowingness and capacity to be happy. You were given this wonderful gift so you could fulfil the purpose of your life on this Earth; to be happy.

Life can make us forget this, because we focus our attention on our fears and become blinded to the love and the happiness that is always inside us. The result is unhappiness through misery, depression, disease and lack.

Choose happiness for a better world

Any focus on misery is a dead end. All this can be changed in an instant. Make a start by making the choice to be happy. There are always possibilities when you choose to be happy. In so doing you will see more clearly that the fears of unhappiness and a bad world are not real. When more of us see this than don't, a tipping point will be reached and want and greed will cease. Jealousies and comparisons will disappear. Wars will end; famine and disease will be wiped out very quickly. In being happy we return to love. What a better way for us all to live on this Earth. We can have all this, and in so doing give friendship, trust, be kind, share, love, help, and be compassionate with each other, instead of being enemies.

You don't have to do this alone

You were never intended to do this on your own. How can you when spirit is part of you. Spirit is the universal field of intelligent energy that is in and around everything. With Spirit everything is possible. Spirit has the power to help you move past any unhappiness. It has the power to help you to be happy! Its wisdom and help is always there for us all, irrespective of what we do, where we are, or who we are. When you make the choice to be happy you join with Spirit and it guides you to fulfil your purpose of being happy and spreading happiness.

Spirit is your life boat

Because of Spirit you are not alone. You have joined with a celestial force more powerful and intelligent than anything you can think of. Spirit is the universal wisdom that acts throughout everything at all times. It loves and helps in ways that you cannot see. We can only see its effects in terms of the beauty and miracle of life. Also, Spirit guides you to others who can help. It is always there. Think of Spirit as being the lifeboat you can sit in where you feel saved. Now you are in a position to help others to escape the perils of the deep. Now you can create more and more happiness. First, get in this lifeboat by making a start on being happy today. When you do this, you are making the choice to be happy, instead of giving away your power in the wrong belief that others can make you happy.

Spirit in action

Because Spirit, like a friend, is always there for you, it will act on your behalf, even if you are unaware of it, or don't even think it is real. Here is an example of the grace of Spirit in action.

As a young man I had gone out with different girls, but never seemed to meet the right one for me. One night I was at the local dance hall when I spotted a girl who I really fancied. And so, I went up to her and asked for a dance. With that she said she had to leave; but I could dance with her friend, if I wished. I stood there feeling silly, thinking that her friend must be right fed up about all this. I then asked her if she wanted to dance. Well, that was it. As I write this we have been married for forty four years, and year after year I realise more and more that she is the best thing that ever happened to me. And so, although I was lousy at choosing a girl, the universe, in its wisdom, picked the right one for me. This is the excellence of Spirits work.

Now you may think this is being lucky. If that is the case then you can say I was indeed very lucky.

But, I have come to know, it is something much more than luck. It is Spirit.

I have learnt:

'If you ask Spirit to help you fulfil a dream, and are steadfast in your belief that it will happen, it will.'

So, when you are up to be being helped, or just going about your life, the universe is always on your side. This is spirit at work. It gives an endless supply of wisdom and love. It has always been possible to be happy and live a Heaven on Earth.

Of course, this is what we were all sent here to have, and to spread this love and happiness to others.

It is you that makes a start on this. When you do this, life just gets better. It is bliss! Enjoy.

With, love and best wishes to you. I hope this has helped you to be happy!

Acknowledgments

Thank you to my wife Vicky. Thank you Vicky Gilgeous for your love and support which, over the years, is always there.

Thank you to my daughters Michelle and Maria. The gift of your lives is always here. How lucky I am to be the proud dad of two such wonderful mothers.

Thank you to Pam Soar. Thank you Pam for being a very good friend and for the help you provide on editing my work. Your natural spirituality is a joy to everyone.

Thank you to all of my students. I love teaching you all. Your feedback has taught me and spurred me on.

Thank you to all of my teachers. Your wisdom has enabled me to draw closer to my joy. In particular I would like to thank Henry Wittka Jezewska, Robert Holden, Wayne Dyer, Deepak Chopra, Guy Finley, A Course in Miracles, Hay House publications and Hay House Radio.

About the author

Vic Gilgeous, PhD, is a teacher and writer on happiness.

His first career was in the Aerospace industry. Starting as an apprentice fitter, he progressed in senior management positions to become controller of Airbus production at British Aerospace.

His second career was in Academia. He taught Management and Happiness at the University of Nottingham.

In these careers, as now in his writing and courses on happiness, he shows that it is possible for us all to live a life that has passion, meaning and happiness.

Other work by the author

For information about having the author run a course, speak to your group or organisation, please contact: vic.gilgeous@ntlworld.com

If the messages and ideas presented in this book have sparked off your interest in this topic and you want to purchase additional copies of *Being happy* or give the book to friends, even strangers, as a gift, go to: Lulu.com, or Amazon.com, or the author at vic.gilgeous@ntlworld.com

Other books by the author are *Right Thinking* and *From Misery to Joy*.

If you wish to purchase these books go to: Lulu.com, or Amazon.com, or the author at vic.gilgeous@ntlworld.com

References

1 Martin E.P. Seligman, Authentic Happiness, Nicholas Brealey Publishing, London, 2003.

2 Deepak Chopra, The Ultimate Happiness Prescription, Rider, 2010.

3 Robert Holden, be happy, Hay House, UK Ltd, 2009.

4 Hafiz, I heard God Laughing, Daniel Ladinsky, Mobius Press, 1996.

5 Hosea Ballou Quotes.

6 Field of Dreams, Directed and written by Phil Alden Robinson, 1989.

7 Carol Adrienne, The Purpose of Your Life, Thorsons, 1998.

8 I Heard God Laughing, Renderings of Hafiz, by Daniel Ladinsky, Mobius press, Oakland, CA, 1996.